the last

MW00698609

"*The Last Ecstasy of Life* is a book to be absorbed at a cellular level, as it speaks to the soul in each of us. I felt a deep sense of joy as I read it. The language and essence is one of love and deep compassion. I know going forward it will be a loving companion on my life journey, offering sustenance, re-hearting, and a constant reminder of what we truly are."

—**Bethan Elsdale, RCST, UKCP Reg, IoB,**
psychotherapist and craniosacral therapist

"This book is groundbreaking. I felt so warmly welcomed into its pages where I was ecstatically inspired by the abundance of life force in death, in dying, in life. Phyllida shows us how to live and die fully through our heart and soul with her deep compassion and wisdom on every page. This book is a soul companion for life and death."

—**Croilan Greta Pattison, MBACP (Snr Accred),**
psychotherapist, teacher of Celtic consciousness, and
guardian of the teachings of the Cauldron of Brigid

"A timely and courageous book, Phyllida's words take us deeply into the mystery of life and death. Understanding death as part of our evolutionary spiritual journey through life, it is seen as a great adventure where the soul is freed to transition into a higher vibrational state of unbounded wholeness, beyond the material world. Phyllida takes a fresh look at the dying process, describing with deep love and sensitivity the final dissolution of the elements and absorption of the soul into the Universal Heart of unconditioned cosmic energy. This is deep wisdom, reassuring, practical, and loving—an essential guide for each one of us preparing for our own conscious death and an invaluable support for those accompanying others making their final passage."

—**Sara Arivanna Trevelyan, M.D.,** psychotherapist, Brennan
Healing Science practitioner, and One Spirit interfaith minister

"I so recommend this book. In beautifully poetic language and poetry, Phyllida Anam-Áire presents an integration of spiritual insights, deep knowledge and understanding of the process of dying, and authentic personal experiences and insights. Her love and compassion, which have brought light and comfort to so many, shine through on every page."

—**Frances de Vries Robbe, R.N.,** esoteric healer and
Access Consciousness practitioner

"Beautifully written and presented, *The Last Ecstasy of Life* contains much information that will be of great help and support to all those who are involved with death and dying—those who are undergoing the dying process, their relatives, friends, caregivers, and supporters. It is also of interest for anyone who wishes to understand more about the great mysteries of life and death. Phyllida writes with a flowing, colourful, and poetic style and covers practical, emotional, spiritual, and esoteric aspects of the experience of dying. This book may raise many questions for the reader, and perhaps one may disagree with aspects of it; but this is good, for without discussion and the free exchange of differing points of view, there can be no advancement of true knowledge. I would recommend this important book, so timely in our world of the chemical and materialistic approach to the phenomenon of death, as a gift of Light in a darkening world."

—**Jacqueline Kemp, BschHon (psychology), ATCL, ALLCM,**
Reiki master and author of *Size Zero and Beyond*

"Phyllida Anam-Áire lets us participate in her own experiences, insights, and amazing understanding about living, dying, death, and rebirth into a new existence. She paves the way to a new consciousness. *The Last Ecstasy of Life* is key to delving deeper into the mysteries of love and overcoming the fear of death. It explains the connections between healing and spiritual evolution and how immensely important it is to heal the psychic pain of our imprints while we are still alive, to be able to face death very consciously in peace, in a final ecstasy."

—**Alannu-Doris Hogger,** healer and psychotherapist

the last
ecstasy
of life

Celtic Mysteries of Death and Dying

phyllida anam-áire

 FINDHORN PRESS

Findhorn Press
One Park Street
Rochester, Vermont 05767
www.findhornpress.com

Findhorn Press is a division of Inner Traditions International

Disclaimer

The information in this book is given in good faith and intended for
information only. Neither author nor publisher can be held liable by
any person for any loss or damage whatsoever which may arise from the
use of this book or any of the information therein.

Cataloging-in-Publication data for this title
is available from the Library of Congress

ISBN 978-1-64411-265-6 (print)
ISBN 978-1-64411-266-3 (ebook)

Printed and bound in the United States by Versa Press, Inc.

10 9 8 7 6 5 4 3 2 1

Edited by Michael Hawkins
Text design and layout by Anna-Kristina Larsson
This book was typeset in Garamond, Avenir and Kells SD

To send correspondence to the author of this book,
mail a first-class letter to the author c/o Inner Traditions •
Bear & Company, One Park Street, Rochester, VT 05767, USA
and we will forward the communication, or contact
the author directly at **seabheann@icloud.com**.

Each earthing
Tells more of
Our story

Each story
Unravels more
And more of our
Mystery

It is with humble devotional heart that I dedicate
this book to the great mystery of Life Itself.

Life Itself has allowed me the privilege of experiencing one tiny
glimpse of its immensity during 77 years, as a divine being,
masked in humanity. It will also allow me the privilege of
experiencing it again when the mask has been removed
and off I go into another experience …

The Final Ecstasy! Wow!

፠

Time and Space
Time and space are the gifts of birth
Timelessness and spacelessness are the gifts of death
We move and dance between the two
Like children playing in fields of corn
Thrashing and teasing the sheafs
As they open to their touch
Would that you could be so easy with life and death.

Contents

Chapter I — The Story Begins   15

Chapter II — The Elements Leave the Body   55

Chapter III – Healing the Family Tree   99

Chapter IV – The Last Ecstasy   119

Chapter V – Questions and Answers   151

Postscript   164

Celtic Blessings and Poems   165

Preface

The thing is, I love writing. My grandfather, from Donegal, wrote in-depth poetry and prose. Poetry, storytelling and singing were all gifts I received from my own family tree and for which talents I am very grateful. Somehow writing a poem or just writing an experience seems to ground the experience for me. It's like the writing of it acts as a witness. You are not alone when you write. I feel the ancestors gather around in stillness watching, taking it all in and I invite them to sit with me and learn, or teach me, as the case may be. Sometimes they form part of my memory and what I forget, they fill in, and this is exciting.

My friend asked me why I wanted to write about death and dying again and wasn't there more to life than dying? I loved the question because in it I found such wisdom. So, is there more to life than dying? I write about death and dying because I believe in the continuum of life whether in physical form or out of it. It is about this that I write; there is more to life than being in a body and there is more to death than being without it.

I believe that life experiences itself just as fully in dying as it does in living because life is not dependent on form. We experience just as deep a connection with life during our dying process as we do in living life daily. The problem is we are socialized into believing that all life comes to an abrupt end in death. In this book, I will share with you my deep belief that life is a preparation for death and death is a preparation for further life and that both are necessary for our integral spiritual evolution.

This book, my fourth, has been "living" in me such a long time, awaiting its expression. I believe books wait in us, they are in step with the timing of things, and I feel now is the time to birth this one. My hope is that you will read it with an open, curious heart—the way I wrote it. Let me know your thoughts when you have read it. I'd like that very much. You see, death is often not talked about with inclusivity or welcome, and I think that is a shame. I believe something very authentic gets lost in the exclusion of death in everyday experiences.

Theosophical teacher Alice Bailey called death "the great adventure" and why would we not want to be involved in the most adventurous journey of our lives?

I'm glad you are with me!

All possible blessings for you, whoever you are, as you live and die in each moment.

Phyllida

Note: All poetry throughout the book that is not otherwise credited was created by Phyllida either as poetry or music.

Introduction

The teachings of the Cauldron of Brigid as a source from which I am inspired advise that if you are lost to yourself so is God lost in you because creation is the out-breath of the creator. Therefore the divine is not only close to us, it breathes us into form, continually renewing us with its essence which is pure, untainted Love. When we have not fully incarnated in earth as form and continually escape to blue paradise instead of being present to now, we stay ungrounded and deep in melancholic longing for the divine or the beyond. We find it difficult to organize our days as we dream of *saol neamhaí*, bodiless existence.

What courage it took to in-body, to take on the cloak of humanness and live the feelings associated with such a state of being. When you find your own individual expression of the divine in earth and live the splendour of your frail vulnerability, then you will have unveiled God, or the divine, not only in yourself but in all of the great mysteries of creation. Our unintegrated parts, our prodigal parts, need to be gathered in so that we can live fully, wholly in the earth and die fully, wholly to earth in the end. In both these great experiences we can manifest the love of the one that lives not only in us but truly lives us. In our Celtic tradition we do not really let go of anything, we integrate it so that it is honoured as part of our experiences in the earth.

Whatever you hold outside your heart becomes a stranger, so welcome all in so that you can be at peace with all, including your earth/ego or conditioned mind. All of you is longing to be welcomed so widen your heart to include the parts of you that you keep out in the cold. Stay close to the cauldron of transformation. Let not your earth/ego mind trick you into believing that the dark is your enemy; there is no enemy save that which you run from.

When we deny a feeling we are denying life in us. We have come to experience life in all its *scealta* "mysteries". There are no good experiences and no bad experiences. These are the labels that the earth/ego mind constructs in order to categorize experience so it is busy attracting the one and avoiding the other. The earth/ego mind is secure in categorizing life because then it thinks it can control it. So imagine, dear one, if you had no clear cut ideologies around the word "experience" but that all that occurred in your life was simply an expression of life?

Dear sisters and brothers, your earth/ego mind sees life as a problem at times. It feels important if it can go about solving problems as it cannot accept what is here and now. This dear earth mind often becomes addicted to finding problems, its own and those of others. Many dear ones spend days worrying about Armageddon as if worrying about it can change things! What can and does change the world is each person living as consciously as they can and by doing so make choices that are life-enhancing and love giving.

Be assured that when you find so-called "solutions" to the so-called "problems" of life, they will be found based on past experiences. Know that the same problems will return many times in different disguises until we move into soul which will move us deeper into the alchemy of our conscious, feeling self. What we project into the universe will find a landing place in ourselves until we finally project a purer love.

Some of you say life is such a problem and it is not fair with such misery everywhere. The Cauldron teaches that life is neutral in essence and it holds no good or bad outcomes for you. The more wisdom and awareness you bring to choices, the quieter your heart will be. If you think that logic and reason alone can bring you peace then give up this thought because it does not bring you freedom. The small, debating rational mind has no knowledge of mystery, nor can it rest in simply bowing to the deeper wisdom of life itself. Reason and logic satisfy only the earth/ego mind, that small, debating, arguing mind.

Please do not accept these precepts if they do not find a resting place in your heart, rather, write your own. Know what you believe and then live that fully but do not become stuck and complacent in your beliefs. Stay fresh and as curious as a child. Use the intelligence of brain, body, feelings and intuition to challenge your beliefs.

It seems that at times we believe that the only intelligence we possess is that of the cognitive mind. When you find a belief that serves you as a growing organism, live that, and know that if you are not free to accept the new then you are not free to live the old. The old beliefs are simply what you inherited and are tribal in their administration, full of Old Testament beliefs such as "an eye for an eye". The freedom of choice is yours. Use it wisely.

I often ask myself what it means to be spiritually intelligent and spiritually healthy. Are they the same? This might be a question you could also ask yourself. For me, spirituality is a living organic expression of life and therefore evolutionary in essence. Spirit is what we are; it is an innate wisdom or knowing that pervades our whole consciousness. It is a spiralling integral continuum whose so-called "truth" transforms and changes as humans transform and grow in consciousness, self-knowledge and intuition. If you still believe all you were taught as a child then you have not truly listened to your own inner tutor, your intuitive self. Know how deeply life welcomes you to live it here and now with joy filtering through the day-to-day experiences.

Whatever does not serve this life in you, does not serve the divine. When we do not honour and care for our spiritual health, we lose sight of what it means to be truly alive in our entire precious embodiment. Whatever serves the creative impulse in our everyday lives and brings a sense of integration to our day is also maintaining spiritual health in us. How often do you give space to your own creative impulses?

> The old scriptures
> Now called into the heart of love's alchemy

And offered on the altar of transformation
Are honoured in the fire
And washed in the tears of a new baptism.

Often we equate happiness with spiritual joy. In order to be happy we need an outer stimulus, something to make us happy. We search for the one and run from the other. Joy is the innate, natural place of spirit in us. Nothing from without can promote it but when we clear the heart of its regrets, projections and revenges, when we heal the inner hurts, joy bubbles up as a natural, quiet presence.

Search not for happy
But have a heart
To swim into the waters
Of your lost self.
When you have learnt to dive
Under the waves of your own tears
You will have reached
The shore of joy.

Scriptures not written from the heart's experience remain as dried-out testimonies to a lesser god. They can never fill the deeper hunger of a living soul.

Together we create a brand new altar, not from the sacrificial innocence of a lamb, but from the sensual clay body of our own longing to be named sacred. No longer satisfied with wine from the dark damp cellar of stale dogma, we now fill the chalice brimful and overflowing with the raw passion of our earthen flesh and blood.

Listen to me, listen to the devotion in our bones… They dance a new Hallelujah to our children's children to the seventh generation.

This is the wine I drink. Come and drink with me… Let us get drunk on benediction. SEÁ.

CHAPTER 1

The Story begins

꙰

For every being that comes
I come in them
For every being that leaves
I leave in them
I am breath
I bring birth
I am decay
I bring death
For every being that breathes
I breathe them
Nothing is ever lost
All is gathered in at last
For every being that loves
I love in them.

What is this "I" that comes? What is this "I" that leaves? Who am "I"? These are the most important questions I have ever asked myself.

The *who* of me is quite clear; it is a personality, a conditioned being that is socialized, culture-ized and religion-ized. This is obvious. As I look around me I see other personalities like me in many ways and yet with various cultural, gender and social differences so as to distinguish us one from another. I see this me as a conglomerate of various psychological, mental and physical components driven by an inward need to survive, thrive and share with the others around me. Naturally, my personal DNA will affect my personality to a degree. Each of us acts out our various patterns of behaving, each with their own individual dysfunctional inheritances as we do the best we can to heal and live together in a community. We have all survived so far with the help of our reptilian brain. Hopefully we can eventually go beyond this state into pure joy.

The more I become aware of my own dysfunctional patterns of interacting, the more congruently I can live. I believe the soul in me is forever nudging me in the way of congruency and authenticity so that gradually, I allow the *what* of me to penetrate the dear boundaries of the earth mind, or the *who* of me, so that I may live a more soul-led life than an earth mind driven one.

As I see it, the more I live from soul, the more grace can infiltrate my conditioned personality until one day I simply live only love. In Malcolm Hollick's book, *The Science of Oneness* he writes, "It is not the atoms of which our bodies are made that makes life real for us but our consciousness; our awareness of the world around us and of our own inner selves."

I add that it is not the conditioned mind full of judgement, guilt and fear that defines me as a human and divine being, rather it is the grace within that shows me this shadow, so that it may be welcomed into the heart and loved into wholeness. I believe what unites us all in this world of differences lies in the awe-filled question "What am I?"

When I consider the immensity of this question I have to bow low in humble submission because the *what* of me and the *what* of you are identical. We are life force itself, imbued with the attributes of immortality and graced with a magnificence that when explored, falls short of explanation and definition. Our dear, finite minds cannot grasp the full immensity of the mystery, nor are we supposed to understand it. This magnificent life force, our collective essence, is pure love. It is neutral in its interaction with created phenomena, meaning it carries no conditions and is of itself genderless and without the emotions to create value systems. Maybe it could be called *love* without the preconditions. Another option could be *compassion*.

From a place of absolute humility we ask for some kind of inner clarity, or even a glimpse of what this power is, so that we may be inspired to sink deep into this *what* of us, despite our very limited intelligence. Indeed perhaps because we try to understand it with this small mindedness, our opportunity to be inspired is curtailed. The Celts believed that creation came about by the out-breath of life force and so it was. Trees and grasses, oceans and mountains all expressed in their own way, the divine purpose within their individual forms. There was no competition. The trees did not look down on the grasses because they were bigger and stronger!

As we human beings walk the world in all our splendour and insignificance, we walk the path of paradox. We carry within the outer covering of human form, the very spiritual DNA of life force which I translate as "Divine Natural Activator". There are times in my own experiences of life when I sit in the most intimate silence absorbed in knowing that:

> I come from breath
> It does not belong to me
> I experience life through breath

Life does not belong to me
I release breath back into life
All there is, is life
And life is not dependent on form.

We are the pure electromagnetic, yin/yang, anima/animus, male/female energy of which the entire universe, the galaxies and all the worlds of created phenomena is made. We human beings come from the very same stuff as the stars, oceans, mountains and trees. Our dense form carries the same strong healing impulses that pulsate and enliven the sap in the tree; the same immense invisible power that seduces all living creatures, from the most powerful to the most vulnerable, to move, live and reproduce on this green-red earth dancing in our blood stream. It vibrates throughout our nervous system singing an ode to love. Any name we give to this neutral force, this abundance, can never attempt to define it, for all naming of it limits it. It does not have a beginning nor will it end. We can only attempt, like children in a classroom with mouths agape at new discoveries, to ask questions and be open to finding the answers within ourselves.

It seems like we live the questions we hold in our imaginations. And the more imaginative we are, the more creatively we will live these questions, until one day, the answers are not important anymore. They breathe and dance in us until we experience the answers in our hearts. For me it is not about trying to understand what life is about, rather surrendering to the questions and letting go of intellectualizing them. Instead of theorizing, I allow the breath to inspire me into experiencing life.

Did you not know
You are the breath
Flowing from the throat of love
Did you forget that we have come
To earth the divine
In your heart and mine.

The Long Journey into Embodiment

Whilst it is so important that we surrender to the mystery and not try to conceptualize or reduce it to our mere intellects, it is also important to make some personal sense of it. Otherwise we become puppets on the strings of weathervane theories that do not help, but confuse us. What you read here are my personal beliefs. When I live deeper experiences in life I can change my beliefs to accommodate them in the here and now. The following have helped me live a more integrated experience of creation.

It seems that fusion processes are to be found everywhere in nature, and more and more complex life is the result of fusion. Louise B. Young, in *The Unfinished Universe* writes, "Life is just a stage in the organization of matter." For example, quarks fuse to create nucleons, nucleons fuse to create more complex atoms, atoms fuse to create molecules and crystals and of course, the egg fuses with the sperm to create life on earth.

John Muir in *Gentle Wilderness: The Sierra Nevada* remarked, "One is constantly reminded of the infinite lavishness of nature; no particle of her material is wasted or worn out. It is eternally flowering from use to use and beauty to yet higher beauty." The miracle of what transpires from the fusion of egg and sperm captures the sacred imagination of both scientist and mystic alike. But what happens before cells multiply and evolve is of the highest importance, and we must rely on ancient wisdom to delve into the mystery of such phenomena.

Plato and Ultimate Reality

Plato, in his book *The Republic* taught that the physical world that we live in is but a shadow of the real world or ultimate reality and that pure reality exists beyond all physicality. His belief was that the physical world is forever changing, always in a state of evolving but not evolved so is therefore imperfect or as Louise B. Young would suggest, "not finished yet!" So it is not difficult to believe that there exists a field of consciousness that is of a higher vibration and higher frequency than the material world, and because it is not subject to our laws of human existence is also beyond suffering and extinction. For, all that has been created must obey the laws of earthing. Only that which has earthed can go through decay and death or transformation and rebirth.

The Auric Body

It seems there is an energetic field that surrounds the internal organs and all physicality. We see that this energetic or auric body is what sustains and supports the physical. When the auric body is not strong in its energy system the physical body collapses. We can therefore deduce that dis-ease begins in the gradual reduction of life force. When our thoughts, which are living organisms, do not uphold a positive vibrancy and sink into depression or lethargy, this affects the physical.

So there is a field that is alive with life force, healing in and of itself and when we encounter and get to the source of it, we are imbued with pure energy and filled with good health. I believe that the Universal Heart, the unconditional cosmic energy is the perfect template of the human heart and is continuously surrounding it with what we call love or harmony. Equilibrium. Unfortunately because of our hearts' woundings, and the unhealed feelings we hold in our physical hearts we cannot always access this grace. But it is the Universal Heart that imbues us with a self-accepting love and a more altruistic love for humanity and creation in general.

Rupert Sheldrake talks about the morphic field or field of resonance. It is an energy field within and around all living organisms. In the Bible we read:

> In it
> We live
> And move
> And have our being.

This life force tunes into our morphic field so that the organism develops in the way suggested by the internal template. This is interesting from the point of view of how we resonate with our own bodies. We talk about resonance with other organisms, but for me it is important to have resonance with my own internal states of being.

For instance when someone has a headache, they can usually stop whatever they are doing, go inside and see what the internal chatter is about and what future or past events are filling their subconscious mind at that time. The dear body might register this disquiet as a headache. Others will find a resonance with their stomachs or other parts of their body. It is as if the body is in sympathy with, and is the messenger of thoughts, and the thoughts register as either happiness or stress and the physical responds with a disturbance in the biology.

Unfortunately we have not had any education on how to resonate with our own body and minds. What a difference it would have made had we been taught that our thoughts affect our physicality. What a difference it might have made in our lives had we been taught that we are the breath of life itself affecting our whole being. If we had learnt at an early age that the healer is in the breath, perhaps our experiences would have been more congruent and authentic, leading to self-honouring, self-monitoring health processes and less possessiveness and judgements of others. And yet we had to learn through not knowing. This is the challenge our souls offered our personalities!

I often forget that whilst I do not possess life, I am fully responsible for my thoughts which produce actions and reactions. I belong with life but it does not belong to me. I have the privilege to be allowed to live it in each breath. My purpose is to experience as fully as I can the amazing grace that each individual breath affords me here and now. This thought challenges me daily and I am not finished yet, but instead am forever in the flow of integral spiritual evolution.

The Electromagnetic Field (EMF)

Scientists differentiate between what they call potential energy (wave form) and standing energy (particle form). If our beliefs (wave energy) actually create our reality (particle energy) then we are surely the authors of our lives, the creators of our own experiences. We resonate with what we have already sent into the universe; we get back what we send out. This is a mighty power for humans to possess. As our individual EMF attracts and finds resonance in the world around us, it also experiences reactions to energies with which we are not in harmony. That is why there will always be people and situations that attract and repel us. Naturally we respond to that with which we resonate, and react to what is repellent, not just to us but within us. Our EMF carries within it every thought, word and action of all our lives. It is individual and also collective. This so-called personal library is also known as the Akashic Records.

The EMF needs a physical body, a "hard drive", in order to download this material. When the physical body is no longer of use to our soul, the body is discarded but not in a crude and unloving way. It has done its work again this time around and knows the natural inner timing of its comings and goings. The soul cannot die. As we know, that energy is immortal and as the individual soul is pure light and pure love, it simply goes home. When it embodies again it joins the magnetic impulses from the last life. It takes up again where it left off, so to speak, and hopefully it becomes more enlightened with each earthing.

However, energy is neutral and we experience it according to our own inner states of consciousness, that is, we experience everything according to our own inner world of associations and references. These inner states are mostly coloured from past experiences and seldom do we have what one might call a "brand new" experience. Psychologist Abraham Maslow called a transcendent experience a "peak experience" whereby "we are in resonance with all creation and therefore we experience everything around us as through the eyes of love and joy for the first time." If this great power of co-creating our lives with the universe is within our EMF then co-creating our own deaths is also within this field of consciousness.

The Resonance of the EMF

When you are in resonance with the "over soul", or over-lighting life force your EMF is said to be in harmony. When one decides to change the energetic patterning within oneself to return to harmony again, changing for example, the defensive-reactive patterning, the outer other responds. The stronger energy will always dominate so, Love is stronger than fear. We are mostly always attracted to people who are friendly and open-hearted. We feel the vibrations bounce off us on the other hand, when people complain and are argumentative. This affects the collective energy field around them. When energy is raised by the transmission of love through the EMF, healing happens and the effect is multiplied. The power of the collective is mighty. This is the power of the community, the communion amongst us.

We say that opposites attract but when the differences are too dramatic, the fields cannot sustain equilibrium. One has to overcompensate to make up for the lack in the other. For example, in families where the father is non-communicative, the mother may overcompensate by talking all the time. This dynamic may also happen when one partner easily accesses their emotions, while the other suppresses them. If both of them can see the problem and make an effort to change their behaviour, there is more chance of a better equilibrium being established. But I have found it is easier to blame the other so that I can be right ... again!

We are all responsible for bringing back a sense of harmony to the earth. Now is the time to really take heed and co-create harmony with one another to bring about the healing of humanity and the healing of all beings. As we heal our dysfunctional instinctual self-patterning of the past—our lower chakra energies of defensiveness and survival, for example—we move up into the mature heart. From there we increasingly emit feelings of compassion and grace. According to Doc Childre, author of *The HeartMath Solution*, our heart EMF extends about 4 metres from our bodies. It is clear therefore, that we are in very close contact with the EMF of others around us. Sharing experiences of love and joy cause photons of light to be emitted through our EMFs which help to spread harmony and equilibrium not only in a community but on the planet itself.

On the other hand, when there is too much electric energy being expressed in driven or frenzied behaviour, this can lead people to behave in an aggressive and impatient way. We notice that when people come together to demonstrate, for example, against war or the government, the collective EMF can turn into one of aggression and disharmony. This is counterproductive to any healing of the situation. It is more difficult to keep the heart open when one is in a defensive mood and the language is aggressive. In an atmosphere of combat and anger, even for so-called good causes, we create a negative EMF and this affects others. When our energy is in harmony and balance, it is more likely to lead to a positive and creative outcome. Whenever we are against anything no matter what that might be, the energy of "I'm against" affects our inner systems, and our hearts contract.

Creating and Re-creating Ourselves

And so it was that an atom went forth and fused with other atoms, and molecules were born from the mighty fusion of yin and yang energy formed from electric magnetic rays which resided at the centre of each molecule. These molecules united in unity consciousness and as time went by, clusters of density ensued. Millions of years later, form was begotten and stars, moons, suns, and galaxies came into being. Such light! Such brilliance from the stars! Such colours from the gasses! Off-shoots from stars dancing in an ever-spiralling vortex of deep vibrational sound!

All forms of intelligence were birthed from the great networking brain of the cosmos, and you were birthed along with all creation.

All was light and colour and sound stirring together in the magnificent boiling temperature of chaos. Stars dying, others appearing, destruction giving way to further growth. Creative forces being flung into possibility. Nothing was haphazard or without purpose. All was one and all was love. And deep in the heart of all creation there was a song finding its tone and melody, and in the song of all creation, we all belong.

This great song infused you with its light, frequency and sound. Its memory is still encoded in each cell of your form waiting to be awakened. And we are waking up. We help one another to wake up and hear the song. Sometimes you will hear it when you are in nature, when you meditate, when you are with children, when you are still or maybe when you are dancing or making love. But we have all heard it and will continue to hear it more strongly when we open our inner ears and eyes. Somehow, our past earth experiences and our present beliefs cause us to believe that we are separate from this great enlightened mind. When we feel separate we close down our inner senses, and open only to the outer ones. We shut down the inner tutor, our intuition, and listen only to the noise of strange teachers. In fear we lock the heart up tight. Maybe these words translated from the Gaelic make sense here:

> tà eagle orm
> mar geall ar do guth dhilis
> naimhaid le mo cluasa
> le moran grá
>
> in fear I shut you out
> because your voice
> now alien to my ears
> frightens me
> with too much mercy

We are so frightened to let love in that we attach ourselves to our personality which would condemn us, rather than listen to the voice of soul that would comfort. In other words, we live the *who* of the fearful personality and sadly, the *what* of us, the divine that we are, cannot find an entrance to enliven us.

We have been literally enlivened by love from the very beginning. Through the medium of electromagnetic resonance before birth, the greater intelligence, our greater intelligence, sent forth the template of the form best adapted to our individual experiences which we adapted in order to heal past misunderstandings and to manifest love. Many people change or shapeshift their form many times in one lifetime. Scientists Carolyn Myss and Bruce Lipton among others, maintain that as thought impulse creates form and one's psychology supports the physiology, our thoughts continue to create our bodies. This may seem far-fetched, but when we look at our worlds we see that we are continuously creating projections of our thoughts. When we do not take responsibility for our thoughts we create havoc both within ourselves and in the psyches of the collective. The act of creation was not a once and for all action; it is a continuous movement of manifestation from consciousness or unconsciousness and back again. By our thoughts we are continuously contributing to either peace or destruction in our world. What am I personally creating at this time in the story of creation? Look around the world, the answer is there.

The Field of Consciousness

Long ago, scientists taught that nothing existed in space, that it was void. Now scientists such as Gregg Braden, Bruce Lipton, Louise B. Young, Ken Wilber et al, let us know that not only is there something in space, but it pervades *all* space. In his book *The God Code*, Gregg Braden calls this something "the field of consciousness". It represents that presence that is neutral, where there is no judgment, no previous story attached. It is a neutral energy which pervades all created phenomena. This field is beyond all judgment of self or another. In other words it is the state of grace, pure innocence, which is the place of neutrality. In this place we can meet one another without the stories attached.

> Oh that we could meet
> naked and new born
> I would take your hand and
> we would dance through a door
> open wide to us
> the key buried beneath the rafters
> never needed again.

Imagine for one moment if we could meet each other, whosoever the other is, friend or so-called enemy and just be together without the judgements! Imagine if we never had to lock our hearts again to any situation, to any experience, that we would and could keep the heart open to the deep alchemy of life and never have to run and lock the heart up ever again.

If life is neutral, innocent and free from agendas for us, then so is love. And if life is all there is, then death must also be neutral. We bring the agendas from the last incarnation each time we come to the earth plane as there is no bookkeeper in the sky tracking my actions and reactions. Of course the more I live in the field of consciousness that Braden spoke about, the more imbued with its higher vibrations I will live. Eventually we will be able to live this more neutral love itself and see only through these clear eyes that are untainted by judgement, jealousy, fear or prejudice.

Imagine truly living life knowing that I am the co-creator with the universe! This is to live in a continuous state of the grace of my enfolding. This is truly to live heaven on earth as we will begin to see that Love is what keeps everything in motion. No longer will we live in fear of disasters and destruction of the world around us. We will have eyes to see that the neutrality of Love

is what creates and re-creates, as it destroys and realigns again…
Always re-creating from the old, always in movement, spiralling
into eternity and back to earth again.

If Love is everything then it must include the very antithesis of
Love otherwise it is not Love but a shallow version of emotionally
charged sentimentality. We need love to be nice and sweet, not an
agent for radical destruction or change. The Sacred Alchemy of
Love's transformation is not for the faint hearted. As Lady Gaga
sang in *A Star Is Born*, "We're far from the shallow now!"

When we bring our sentimental or preconceived conditions
to any relationship, we are not prepared to heal into a deeper,
more expansive experience of ourselves. The other, whatever or
whoever that might be, is but a reflection of my own inner states
of being: as within, so without.

The old wisdom advises us to live with what is natural and
to learn from nature so that we might be more accepting of
life and follow our natural rhythms instead of living in states
of separation. The natural rhythm of life is pure love. And we
have to grow into this love. It is a long journey from love that
is based on conditions and expectations to love that is not
dependent on preferences or past associations. It is brand new,
therefore scary!

Pure Love is the energy which holds and maintains all creation
in sacred equilibrium and balance. It is orderly and also forever in
a state of evolutionary growth. When we reach the stage of living
from this essence, we are never the same again. Sacred Alchemy
will have transformed us and we will see through the eyes of
Love. This Love does not judge or condemn as its core is the
Universal Heart, the heart of compassionate energy. It can hold
the suffering of the world as it is not emotionally involved. At
times people will say to me, "Phyllida, how does your heart hold
so many sad and grieving stories from people?" The secret is this:
I do not hold this pain in my own human heart. My heart just
has to stay open. The Universal Heart of compassion cradles all
with its powerful energy.

When my small, darling human heart has been widened by grief, and feelings have been expressed from the heart, then something huge happens. We begin to realize that at the other side of integrated grief is fullness of life. And at the other side of integrated fear is joyful reaching inwards, to the Love that fires us. And then comes the reaching out, deeper and deeper into the world, fully animated by soul.

This poem, "Shape Changing", brings expression to these feelings:

> Only in the shape changing of my heart
> Only in the trembling of its walls
> Falling open
> Open to itself
> To everything, to all
> Only in the sacred burning of every desire
> Ashed back to you
> Only in the dance of this carnival
> Can I roar into my song
> Of freedom.

The Universal Heart in Life and at Death

We have given you teachings about the Universal Heart as you live your daily life. Of course daily living also includes daily dying. This daily dying is part of *life* itself, and when you are not able yet to acknowledge this truth, the life you live will be without vitality because vitality comprises both letting in and releasing with each breath. Holding on or forgetting to receive are both destructive to life force and detrimental to our physical, mental and spiritual health, including our emotional health and the health of the collective.

As the Universal Heart is the template for the organ of the physical heart in life, it is also the overshadowing angel or aura present when the heart is struggling to maintain its presence in the sacred dying process. If one has lived life with fullness and honour, the Universal Heart will have expanded their inner and outer awareness to a great extent. Those who have not recognized the presence of the Sacred Heart will have problems letting go into the full spectrum of life that the spiritual heart offers. When the physical heart has not dealt with the grief and sorrowing of loss during life, it will feel the heavy burden of unshared pain at death and will be unable to journey into so-called glory into the pure light that this heart emits. To be able to move into the Universal Heart one has to be willing to open wide to the unexpressed feelings dwelling in the physical heart. To do this one needs the help of a compassionate witness. Here is a poem about expressing grief:

> and in your sorrowing
> become one with the earth
> and howl your nakedness
> to the wounded leaves in winter
>
> do not say spring is not far off
> but keep company
> with the songless bird
> as she mourns with toneless throat
> the death of her children

So we are advised to sound our grief into the earth and stay until it is finished. The advice, "do not say, spring is here," can be said in another way: do not hurry grief. Grief is a gift we give ourselves when we allow the physical heart to mourn its losses.

This opening into grief is the most important part of recognizing the presence of the Universal Heart for, like joy, which cohabits with grief, it is always there, awaiting the unveiling and expressing of grief to reveal its presence.

When we move into the Universal Heart something happens in our own hearts. They feel the support, the unbelievable unconditional love that this Sacred Heart bestows. It opens us to possibility and if we have not dealt with our unfelt passions and emotions, this opening causes us to rebel and hold on even more. The language of *this* Love is not sentimental, nor is it sweet. Rather, it confuses the reasonable mind and has no thought for concepts or logic.

This opening into the Sacred Heart transforms us for life. Literally what was painful before, is now bearable; what was bearable, is integrated and even loved. It seems that the love of the Universal Heart turns us upside down and inside out. This poem speaks to this chaos. It stirs us in the cauldron and appears to show no mercy… What an alchemist!

Spiralling

Love's language confuses
The tired mind cries out
Be reasonable
Or, I cannot keep you company
Oh beloved, you make me crazy
You turn my world around
So night is day and day is night
Is it your intention then
To stir all things to chaos
To sing a page of straight lines
Into a circle dance
Of madness
Oh watermelon in my veins,
I will enter your spiral
I will lose my mind in your kiss
I will dizzy my head
And emerge wide-eyed
Howling joy.

When we speak of love we confuse it at times with those other words, desire or attraction. Both desire and attraction are mortal phenomena whereas the Love of the Universal Heart for our own physical heart is immortal and non-phenomenal and travels with us after the physical heart has ceased to work. It cannot die as it has never taken form, as it is an energetic being.

The Universal Heart infuses the physical heart with strong emanations of electric energy to ensure its stability and harmonious pulsatings. It has not been subject to conditioning. It contains within it *the pure energy of the elixir of life itself that sustains all living things.* It is the over-lighting energy throughout creation and in it we live, move and experience our being. It shape-changes into the form it inhabits, and flows through and is the internal mechanism through which, and in which, the fusion of certain chemicals and fluids come together to imbue inertia with *life.* This Love is creative and cannot be owned.

So what happens at death? When we are dying the electromagnetic energies that sustained form begin to slacken, begin to weaken. The sacred five elements dissolve as the dear form can no longer contain them. It has another journey to take. This is natural. When the physical heart has flatlined with the brain, then the energies of the human heart come to an end. That does not mean that the Universal Heart also stops operating. Depending on the openness one had to living a full life, the Universal Heart widens in them. If the human heart had never opened because of fear of being hurt, or fear of making a mistake and so on, the aura that surrounded this human heart is thin, with little energy left. This is just the way it is.

If someone comes into a room and they are full of life force one senses this. These are the emissions of energy from the Universal Heart that expand and go beyond form. When one is weak and not so filled with life force, the energy from the Universal Heart is also weak. We are the carriers of these great heart emissions. It does not force itself on any form, but those who welcome it and express heart-life are filled moment by moment with this grace.

When flatline has happened, at time of death the unexpressed feelings from the human heart flow into the Universal Heart and lower the vibrations more. As the thoughts that flooded the heart before death take prominence and appear as real phenomena, the dead person deals with the unfinished business as if it were real. If self-judgment makes them look back in regret then this is what their reality is. The energy from the Universal Heart will not rescue but will help the person to show compassion for themself. If, while on earth the person did not accept help or guidance they will continue to struggle and suffer. Prayers and mantras at this stage are very important for the dead being. As above, so below continues to be the continuum and holy beings who have passed on may try to help. If however, pride stood in the way of receiving help on earth, this personality trend will continue through the energy field.

On the other hand, if the person had lived a full and responsible life, opening into feelings of grief and joy and in deep connection with the Sacred Heart in them, the story is other. The Universal Heart opens to them more and more as the dying process continues and grace and compassion, joy and ecstasy flood the psyche. Such a one is said to die in the arms of love literally. The Universal Heart surrounds them with bliss and all that they have lived is in one moment seen as grace. Even the sad and grieving times are seen as grace-filled. The light that is said to be at the end of the tunnel of NDEs (Near-Death Experiences) *is the Universal Heart, full of illumination and bliss.*

But dear one, why wait until the dying process before getting in touch with and listening to the teachings from your own Sacred Heart?

Let the light surround your own heart with the spirit of pure Love that seeks nothing from you, that wants nothing from you and needs nothing from you. In the compassion of *this* heart you have always been enough as it only knows honouring. It will not force you to accept it, nor will it reject you for not opening to it. It sees your pain and will not break your will. It fully respects your decision. Not only does it respect your decision, it welcomes it, as it is neutral in its flow of loving healing energy.

Let us open to love
Let us open to joy
Let us open to soul

For that is what we are.

The words of this song also touch me:

Deep in the heart of all creation
There is a song
And in the song of all creation
We all belong

Deep in the heart of all creation
There's only love
And in the heart of all creation
We are that love.

How extraordinary to believe that we are the manifestation of Love on earth. If so, how am I expressing this pure life force in my daily experiences? Is it even possible to live divine Love?

I live as a stone lives
Just gathering stories
I live as a stream lives
Just letting them go
I live as a tree lives
Sure of my standing
I live as a bird lives
Just singing my song

I live the silence in the wind
I live the silence between words
I live the silence in the seas
I live creation deep in me.

I admire the way stones, for centuries, just sit there in total stillness and listen to stories. This word "listen" is so important. I ask myself "Do I listen to ask questions, or do I listen to hear?" How many times people add their own agenda or their own story when another tries to share a grief or hurt. Some of us are so self-absorbed that each story we listen to ends up becoming our own although the initial request was to listen. Imagine just listening, offering full presence and never offering either advice or suggestion. Imagine not always adding our own story to that of another when they try to relate part of their life journey to us. Imagine being fully here and now present for another. This is grace.

When I look at the trees in my garden, I see how they fully express life in their changing seasons. The wind blows and they surrender. The sun pours down on them and they are not disturbed. The snow covers their nakedness and they mould themselves to its cold covering. Autumn sings her lament and the coloured leaves drop down, down into the dark waiting clay. This is done in silent wonder as the tree bows to the sacred laws of nature hidden in her DNA. And all the while the tree is sure of her standing; sure of her place in the family of nature.

And the stream helps to integrate the stories by gently carrying them out to be part of the sea. It is as if the stream is there to simply assist us in our continuous flow of experiences. The small, insignificant occurrences of everyday life, permitted their own timing, being honoured and then being integrated in its all-absorbent waters. Imagine your story being cradled in the depths of the ocean having been brought there by a tiny stream!

I ask myself how sure am I of my standing in the earth? How difficult is it for me to welcome and then surrender my tears, my years, my insecurities and my fears? How difficult is it also to welcome and surrender my joys, my delights, my choices, preferences, my loves and my talents. In other words how sure am I of the *what* of me? The divine *I am*?

I imagine whether I could live my life as a bird lives, just singing my song, living my divine purpose and whether that could be enough? Maybe that is how I would live this divine life if I lived the divine me. Then there would be an end to all struggle and suffering for I would see life and death experiences through the eyes of Love with nature as my spiritual healer and guide.

> At 3 pm today
> I witnessed a death
> A slow falling into earth
> And the oak leaf
> Showed me that dying
> Need not be a struggle
> But we in our struggle
> Make such a deal of it.

God as Personality: A *Who* God

It seems to me, that as long as we attribute gender to divine life force we limit it. Indeed, all naming limits it to our human associations. God in and of itself does not take form. The beams from the sun reach earth and lighten it, but the sun does not ground itself in a clay body; it remains forever the fullness of itself whilst infusing all creation with the warmth of its presence.

It is true that our foremothers and forefathers prayed to the Sun God and in some places it was celebrated as an all-powerful masculine and in others as the life-giving feminine. It was a source of great power and life depended on its radiance. Although they gave it a gender it was without a personality. We love to personify God as it feels more human and therefore it becomes more reachable when we do so. But it also imbues it with human attributes and this is the problem.

People speak of Mother God, Father God and the feminine attributes of God and it's true we have had the powerful influence of an almighty patriarchal God for the past 5000 years and it is difficult to de-gender. The fact that God cannot love nor can God hate may be anathema to many who for years had prayed to a God that they believed might listen to their neediness and grant them release. When the prayers are not answered as their personalities want, they feel that they are not good enough or that God does not hear them, so they try harder.

To be an adult means we have to take responsibility for our own incarnations and for many this is not an option. As long as we have a belief that allows us to stay spiritually immature, grasping unworthily for the crumbs of God's love and begging for release, we remain immature, and our spiritual evolution is sadly curtailed. We become separate from the inner world of true devotion to the divine in us and in all creation, and continue reaching upwards to a father or mother who might one day deign to look upon us in mercy. This philosophy keeps us victims and small, and is not true humility. It is a form of self-negation and promotes the helplessness of victim consciousness. I write these words with some kind of authority, because at the beginning of the 1960s I spent some years as a Catholic nun in a convent in Ireland. I left the convent because I needed to return to the world and rename and reclaim the sacred for myself.

Rename the Sacred

I love the word "sacred", as it is about sacrament. It seems to me that in living and in dying we need to rename the sacred for ourselves if we are to live an integral life of integrity and devotion. When I left the convent, I was asked if I had found God there. My answer was as follows, "No, I did not find God in the convent as a nun. I found God when I looked into the eyes of a horse two weeks after I left the habit." The habit was to name the divine in accordance with the dogma and commandments of a church only. I began then to rename the sacred for myself from an experiential truth. People often see the sacred through their children. Walking in nature, eating delicious food, poetry, playing with our children, dancing and singing, making love, are all graces we can name as sacred encounters with life itself. These experiences open us up to different states of being and have a positive effect on our psyches.

It seems to me that for too long we have been indoctrinated according to what the hierarchy of the Church deemed sacred or profane. Like small children we have believed that in order to live a righteous life we had to name ourselves sinful beings, beg forgiveness for our wrongdoings, accept the inappropriate guilt, live in separation from grace—"Lord I am not worthy"—and believe we were never good enough, no matter how hard we tried to be like Jesus. On the whole, we begged for forgiveness from a father who seemed not to listen, and for many of us this was the replica of an earthly father, the absent father.

I lived this half-life of victim as a young Catholic girl in the 1950s and truly embraced it as a nun who had offered her young immature life to Jesus as a sacrificial offering so that he might rescue her. For me at the time, the possibility of finding refuge within myself was impossible. We learnt early on in our Catholic education that whatever was earth-born was sinful and all that was formless, without a clay body, was good and holy. It was difficult to see how the divine and mere clay could possibly co-exist in humanity. The sacred was also directional and that direction was upwards. The profane took a downward route. Humanity was both earth born and into earth interred. Our light shadows, our golden selves, our divinity was never owned and never integrated, nor was the body deemed sacred. Women's bodies in particular were seen as impure, ungodly and agents of sin. Therefore we kept looking outside ourselves for God. The hierarchical trajectory of holiness from Pope to parish priest persisted throughout. These men were our intermediaries with God without whose instructions one could not live a good and holy life.

Death also presented us with many problems as heaven or hell were the options afforded us, with purgatory as an in-between consideration if we had been half good! I sat at many a bedside of dear people believing they were going into the eternal flames of hell because they were not perfect. My own parents died with such a terrifying belief. On her death bed my mother said to me, "Your way to God is love, mine is full of fear." Those words pained my heart for a long time.

So what is it to rename the sacred in our everyday lives so that we can live our lives with joy and die in grace and freedom? I often ask myself what needs to be made sacred again in me. I am no longer a sacrificial offering!

So how do I name myself in the family of things? Do I name myself sacred or not worthy?

What is it to name myself sacred, holy? For me, it is to be made whole; a fully incarnated woman with identity and a personality infused with grace, living authentically and joyfully from soul. Being self-responsible for choices and knowing that all and everything in my world is only information for me. How I interpret this information has to do with my own healed or unhealed psychology, from an integrated or disintegrated personality point of view. If I live daily with the Universal Heart pulsating alongside my human heart then I can literally embrace the suffering of the world and never burn out or tire from offering presence, because I will be vitalized by the streams of grace I receive from this overflowing chalice of compassion.

I see life itself as a sacrament of whole-making. Life contributes to our whole-making and to our holiness all the time. It is a continuous spiral affecting our spiritual evolution. And this spiritual evolution must also include our biology as it is not separate from our spirituality.

Shadowed Self

It would seem that what truly needs to be integrated in us as human beings, is the shadow self. It is asking not only for integration but for it to be made holy and to be deemed sacred. This may surprise many but until the shadow and lost self is welcomed into the house of love within, it will remain a stranger. The personality that has been conditioned and socialized has had to abandon itself in order to be accepted and loved, and this abandonment begins in childhood. I often remind people that when they do not welcome the shadow parts of themselves they actually abandon themselves. When we refuse to accept our fears, jealousy and arrogance as part of our holiness we are rejecting ourselves. When we send our unhealed emotions out there in the world we are actually denying parts of ourselves and we then see them in others.

For some years I blamed my father and mother for my confused existence. It was appropriate and good to externalize the rages in a safe therapeutic setting and eventually get to a place of integration and see what I had taken on to heal this lifetime. Many of us who have felt unloved as children behave in strange ways in order to be loved. Some of us learned to prostitute our own beliefs for another and to subsequently emotionally abuse ourselves by saying yes when we meant no. We agreed to situations that were hurtful to us in order to keep the so-called "love" of another. It is therefore necessary for us to truly see today, how we neglect our own hearts so that another approves of us. We will give our hearts away and victimize ourselves for a few moments of approval from another. This does not help our whole-making, yet we continue the non-holy practice until one day we see that it is not working and we need help. This is the beginning of grace.

Here are words from a song I composed in the 1980s:

> I didn't know
> They never said
> I never heard
> Anyone say
> I love you
> You're special
> And so I never felt ok.

Then I grew up
And I was seven
I learnt new ways
To make them say
I love you
You're special
But still I never felt ok.

Now I am older
And I'm wiser
I tell myself everyday
I love you
To me you're special
And now at last I feel ok.

Another beautiful poem created by Alison McLaren fits here:

Oh frozen child,

May the tears that you let flow
never fail to amaze you with their beauty
gently gently medicine woman.
May the courage that you show in life's trials
find its way into your feet
and with this trail blaze your own path
gently gently strong woman.

I don't know where I am going
or if I'm going to fall
all I know is that I must take
that first step to walk in beauty
for the one and for the all.

They say the path less travelled
is the hardest one of all

but if I stay here stuck—
I surely won't win at all.

If this self-love, this courage to step into the unknown is not nurtured by the heart of wisdom it can easily fall between the cracks of selfishness and self-absorption. I find that not many people actually understand self-love. They equate it with self-indulgence or some romantic version of self-acceptance, such as looking in the mirror and repeating the words, "I am beautiful just as I am", eventually to be followed by, "but I'm not, I'm horrible." These statements need to be taken seriously and applied at the right time. Otherwise they are cosmetic and do not form part of a secure belief.

Self-love is not about fulfilling my wants and desires that were not met by parents. I used to hear people say, "Well, my inner child never got to play, so I'm going to play all I can." Unfortunately these dear people looked quite foolish as adults behaving like children or teenagers. Another statement I have heard a few times is, "My inner child never had money so I'm going to buy myself a new car—the most expensive I can get." That is the child wanting and needing and it will never be satisfied as material things do not satisfy the heart longing for true acceptance and compassion.

Self-love has to have a strong, disciplined base if we are to grow up into contented loving and lovable people. If we are too emotionally attached to our inner child she will never attain inner authority or self-worth. It is a long journey finding one's inner self, one's vulnerability, one's fragility, one's strength and good discipline accompanied by consistency. We needed these core attributes as children, but most of us did not have access to them.

Earth/Ego Mind and Soul

The earth mind or ego stems from the concept of "I". "I" being different, other than "you" and "them". Unfortunately, this "different from" eventually becomes a judgement, eg., I am separate from you, I am better than, not as good as, taller, smaller, holier, etc. than you/them etc. The ego does not like the concept of *us* together. It likes to maintain the consciousness of separation.

Freud in his wisdom at the time, the early 1900s, decided that human beings operate from within the psychical triad of the Id, often spoken of as the unconscious; the Ego as the subconscious; and the Superego as the conscience. Although they appear as three different states in themselves, they are actually aspects of the psyche facilitating a deeper understanding of *same*. I imagine Freud's description somehow akin to the Holy Trinity in Christianity, ie., one God with three aspects.

When we view the earth mind/ego through the lens of the child, parent and adult perspective, the Id was seen as the child, needy and wanting, not taking responsibility etc., and the Superego as the critical parent, often controlling and attached to social norms and regulations. The Ego came between them both in an attempt to balance the psyche, to try and behave as an adult. But it was influenced of course by Id and Superego. I have also seen a similarity between Freudian belief and the victim triangle. Again, a triad of victim, rescuer and perpetrator. The child portrayed as victim, Ego as rescuer and Superego as perpetrator or controller. I have also interpreted Id as the place of reptilian consciousness, the beginnings of our evolutionary journey into humanness. That magnificent instinctual reptilian self that helped us survive thus far in our human development.

The Superego in us tries to keep us in line! Keep us good and right. That is how it believes we are safe. When we break the rules, we are burdened with guilt and often shame which again, are attributes of childhood. Religion, I believe, manifests the Superego as it tries to mould us into what it believes is good for us and for others. It condemns us when we do wrong. Superego is also attached to creating hierarchies, which creates so-called order in society.

So, when we speak of ego we speak of our identity, the *who* of us, ie., how we see ourselves in relation to and in comparison with others. These views come from childhood and are responsible for the ways in which we built up a strong earth/ego survivor in us. By the age of six this amazing ego-self had grounded itself in our psyches. Unfortunately most of our egos have stayed stuck at this age and have not been introduced to the guidance and refinement of soulfulness. I have often seen in myself that my reactive and less loving personality has had its roots in the building of my earth/ego mind.

So we see that earth/ego mind comprises three components which may appear to be separate variables but they are not. In fact they give energy to each other and support each other to evolve whilst we are here on earth. They are energetic components of the earth mind. Their job is to help me survive on earth and support me in order to maintain relationships with others, though those relationships may not be entirely authentic. There is no part of me that truly opposes me. In addition, my dear earth/ego mind can be a wonderful help in my becoming more and more conscious when I know how to work with it, not against it. This includes not seeing it as bad or wrong.

And there is another more congruent way we can begin to view ourselves and our relationships which, with the cooperation of the earth/ego mind, can heal us and help us to go beyond a consciousness of sheer survival.

Source or Core Aspect of Self Is Soul

Although the ways of the Oversoul (which is the core energy, ie., Soul or perfected electromagnetic energy in all created phenomena) often called *Life Force* or *God,* may seem to be in opposition to those of the earth/ego mind, they all co-exist in the safe holding of the *Universal Heart*, which is compassion, an aspect of Oversoul itself. All is held in the sacred cauldron of Soul Compassion and there is no judgment. There is also no hierarchy because Soul is a neutral energy, carrying in it no dualism. Therefore it cannot compare nor is it competitive.

In actual fact, if we delve deeper we see that not only is Soul *not* more spiritual than the earth/ego mind, they co-exist as *one*. They are two sides of the same coin. There is no war between earth/ego mind and Soul. The war exists when we separate them, when we divide and try to conquer. This is the fall from grace when we create barriers between the two, when we judge one holier than the other, when we strive for one and discount the other, or when we deem one good and the other bad. This creates war inside us and outside in the world around us. Our goal, if there is one at all, is complete integration of soul and earth mind.

And here is when the shadow comes into play. We try to hide the so-called unacceptable aspects of our personality in order to show only the good and acceptable parts. This does not mean the shadow aspects disappear. They get hidden deep in the subconscious only to appear at another time. They cannot find healing in the subconscious. They must be brought into the light of consciousness to heal. When we do not heal our individual shadow self we lay burdens on the shoulders of others and they have to "carry our cross". We contribute to collective unconsciousness which of course plays havoc in the world.

It takes courage to look at the shadow self and when the earth/ego-self is loved enough, is safe in our hearts and not judged by us, it can reveal our disintegrated and fragmented parts and find healing. This is why self-love is all important. When we see our own innate innocence, pureness, we look out through these eyes and see only innocence without. The soul can help us in this. It is the light that shines on the shadow welcoming it home within the soft cradling of the Soul's compassionate energy.

But it will not insist. It does not have an agenda for us. It only asks us to have experiences on earth and balance the energy from the incarnation before so that equilibrium can be restored at last and all may be one. As it was in the beginning, is now, and always will be. It is just that the dear personality is a bit slow, asks too many conceptual questions and gets in the way of unity consciousness.

I see my individual soul as a wonderful guide for me as it shines a light on my shadows. This is a great grace because whilst the shadows are in hiding in the sub- and unconscious, they cannot be healed. They can only be healed when my earth/ego mind feels safe enough to show them, one at a time.

Soul in us is forever guiding us in the direction of self-love, responsibility to the self and transformation of the self.

When we decide to live in the energy of soul, something happens in relation to the earth/ego mind. Shifts of consciousness begin in the ways I describe below and in many other ways.

I begin to:

1 See myself as I am ... innocent.
2 See others as they are ... innocent.
3 See the world around me as it is ... innocent.

When I invite Soul into my earth/ego mind the following might occur:

1 I enter the cave of the earth/ego mind ... I begin to redefine myself to myself and to others—not as my ego defined me.

2 I tell the story that was up until now not heard ... My feelings are honoured and I am witnessed in a good way which redefines my authenticity... I am not looking for praise, acclaim, to be noticed etc. My shadows come to the light of day. They are invited.

3 What I deemed as truth falls away and I create my own beliefs, new credos about me that serve me and the world around me.

4 I am more attentive to small things. I live more in the present moment and see how things are now rather than what they were in the past. *I am not defined by my wounds any more.*

5 I integrate all blame, shame in myself. I welcome them in to the warmth of my warmed heart. There is nothing to forgive and no one has to forgive me of anything. I create rituals for/ to my ancestors and I accept my/our innocence.

6 My ego is safe in my heart. Fear is cradled in peace. It does not have to shout or dictate any more. My defence reactions have lessened because there is no war raging inside. My earth/ego mind has less and less to do, so it keeps quiet in the shelter of my own heart, surrounded by universal love.

7 The past is gathered safely into my heart as is the entire universe and as I rename the sacred in my own life, I name the Sacred in Myself.

Now I have owned my Divine Self. Now I am free. *SEÁ.*

Many times I will enter this cave of the underworld within me. Just know dear one, that each time I re-enter I come out more *integrated*, more united in myself. This process of spiritual and integral evolution is a continuous experience and in the end, it is truly a joy to enter the cave because we will be simply learning more reasons to love our self and all creation with a purer love.

Alchemy of Integration

The true alchemy of integration is about calling ourselves home; calling all the prodigal parts to sit at the hearth of our own sacredness and welcoming our own hearts to the feast of life itself. It is about marrying the personality with soul and experiencing the whole-making of our own integration. The holy marriage is just that: the fusion of earth mind or ego mind with soul. This is not for the fainthearted. This is the work of those who choose to heal patterns of dysfunction from the past so when the *what* of us has fully infiltrated the *who* of us we will find true freedom.

The dear personality will have been transformed by grace into love. Then there will be no more self-abandonment for we will feel the pure energy of love fill our hearts. The physical heart will be infused with grace from the Universal Heart and the joy already present will overflow into the earth so that even the trees and grasses will rejoice. This is the true path to enlightenment for then the cells in the body will light up with the energy of the cosmos as each nucleus will shine forth the life force residing there. At death this light will shine gloriously as the physical cells dim, the sacred aura emitted will flow through the whole physicality like a strong, awakened dancing flame.

As I have written before, life is not dependent on form. It takes form so that it might experience physicality. When the form dies, life continues in another dimension free from form. The lighter our thought vibrations have become, the more likely those thoughts will manifest in the here and now, which will affect our dying process.

For instance when we die, the thought vibrations will have heightened and manifestation will be instantaneous. If we decide we would like to be beside a beautiful waterfall, the waterfall appears. But it is not of substance like an earth waterfall, it is an auric, energetic template of the earthed version. The same happens with people. We can imagine being with a dead relative and they can appear in the moment of intention. Resonance will attract what we desire. This phenomenon will be touched upon later in the book. It is enough to say here that we can learn whilst in body to quicken our vibrations so that we can have a closer contact to our soul energy so as to not be so dulled by dense materialism.

What Is It to Die?

As it was in the beginning is now, and always will be. Life is forever in movement, moving in a spiralling dance. Coming, evolving and leaving, always in the trajectory of growth and integral spiritual evolution. You might say that not everyone lives a spiritual life and not everyone dies a spiritual death. This is the lie! All creation comes from source and that source is spiritual. It is the very essence at the heart of all creation. People are often described as not being spiritual because they appear to live a very materialistic life. We are all spiritual beings and some are just not aware of this or simply choose to put the emphasis on materialism. *There is no other life to live save that of a spiritual one.* In our judgemental minds we criticize those who are not on a "spiritual path", yet we announce to all that *we* are!

It is how we experience this energy whilst in bodies that creates the difference. Some will listen more to the hurt personality and follow it which leads to more and more unhappiness as it denies the wounds of childhood. Some dwell on the wounding of childhood and that becomes their reality. Others determine to be free in their personalities and do all they can to heal the inner chaotic world. There is no judgement of our choices; it is just the way we are as individuals at various stages of our awakening. There is no hierarchy of spirituality and this again is difficult for us to imagine. We love to "pigeonhole" people. We might say "So and so is not spiritual. She does not meditate, she drinks. She is not holy." This, to me, is spiritual arrogance and it is untrue. We seem to judge what is holy and what is not according to our own inner critic and self-judgements. Of course these criticisms have had their roots in a patriarchal religion that did not serve the living hearts of men and women, condemning the so-called sinner to hell and affording the so-called good to a life with God.

When we choose to be more conscious of how we are in the world we can live with much materialism and when we are not attached to it, it can be the means of our spiritual evolution. It is when we attach ourselves to it and identify ourselves by what we have or who we imagine we are, that the problem begins. And the problem is that our internal world is ill-nurtured whilst our outer world is literally stuffed. I so enjoy colourful clothes and good chocolate. I also like to polish my nails! This gives me pleasure but some people would frown on this and call it worldly.

I call it fun! Should the colourful clothes, the nail varnish and the chocolate be taken from me, I would not miss any of it. There is no clinging to these things, and I don't identify myself as needing them to be full of joy.

As Above, So Below

Because I have experienced some Near Death Experiences, death therefore holds no fear for me. I see it as the natural transformation that I see in nature. The four seasons show me how to be in the present moment and to enjoy the wonder of breathing in and out, in harmony with them. Death for me will be simply to take off the outer mask and live freely without the heaviness of a dense body. To be free is to live pure joy in whatever field of consciousness I choose. The dear body can rest in the earth again whilst the *what* of me, having infiltrated my personality will be free to join source again; the prodigal gone home.

When I leave this world and enter another, how I have lived this precious incarnation on earth will be important to me. Does living consciously then determine how I die, or can I decide at the very end to change my attitudes and beliefs to enable me to die what for me will be, a happy death?

I believe that most of us will die as we have lived and for each person that will be different. No two people have the same birth story and no two people have the same death story. What might be deemed a happy death for one might not be for another. It has to do with consciousness during life and consciousness at death, and naturally it has to do with the culture regarding death and dying at that time. This I feel is important.

We are guided by our cultural and spiritual evolutionary progression. For instance, for someone dying in 1980, it was accepted that they would be resuscitated many times and would be urged to stay alive. Many times I heard nurses and doctors say, "We did all we could and we lost her in the end. I'm sorry," as if the life and death of the patient was held in the hands of the medical staff. This sense of failure infiltrated the psychology and *modus operandi* of many a hospice at the time. The physical must be kept alive, apparently because the idea of another aspect of life outwith the physical was just too difficult to comprehend. We still encourage the dying to "fight the disease" or to "battle with death". This combative language does not honour the soul in its timing.

It was seen as a form of love of the dying to keep them "alive" as long as possible even though the soul had almost vacated the form. Staying "alive" in such a way, with the support of machinery was deemed better than death. For whom? Likewise when we urge a dear one, (mostly for our own selfish reasons) to keep fighting, this is such an intrusion on the life departing. Hopefully we are being more and more educated in the ways of dying. I have witnessed many dying people expressing feelings that they had let their family down by not getting better. "They are praying for me and God is not hearing them," said one elderly man. He was ready to die but the pleadings of his family that God might return him to them in good health was causing him pain.

Many people in the past who experienced the awful ordeal of being resuscitated many times manually and by means of machinery, died at a time when such methods and such beliefs were prevalent. However the soul intelligence of the dying person knew all about that and their choice of having incarnated at such a time and with such beliefs. It was all part of the incarnational soul choice, so one must not feel ashamed or guilty if one's parents had such experiences at death. We have learnt much in the meantime and therefore our compassion for ourselves will be greater at the time of dying as our knowledge of the dying process will have evolved.

Now that we have more spiritual education regarding the energetic processes involved we can choose another reality; one that includes a consciousness towards the needs of the departing soul and less emphasis on interfering in the sacred process of dying. As I shared before, I believe that life is a journey of spiritual evolution and death is no less so. In the next twenty or thirty years we will see the vast difference in how we as a world culture, view the earthing and dying processes.

The Story Is Ending, or Is It?

I believe I will live forever because in other dimensions, time is obsolete. The dear physical being will dissolve and the personality, if it has not integrated the story of its experiences and if the internal marriage of soul and earth mind has not happened, will find its own dimension in which to live out its story. If it has united to life force or soul it will have fused into one consciousness and will travel together to one of the many mansions that Jesus spoke of when he said, "In my father's house there are many mansions." These mansions or dimensions have been generated by the continuous thoughts and consciousness through the life span and especially during the last breaths. If the personality has not been united with soul it may choose to manifest on the earth plane as an astral being still choosing earth life. There is no judgement. It is about harmony and obeying the laws of spirit. On the earth plane we have to obey the sacred laws of the universe and in death we still have laws of spirit to follow through. It is not about judgement, rather it is about balance and equilibrium.

And our story begins again and again and again.

Questions to Explore

- What does the word God mean to you?
- Do you need a God? If so, why?
- What is spiritual health?
- How do you rename the sacred in your life?
- What do you believe the world is made up of?

CHAPTER 11

The Elements leave the body

❧

I belong
with the great eternal elements
that electrified my passion
magnetized my dreams
to people
nature
places
stars and primroses.
the now faded blood in my tired veins
will flow like a mighty torrent again
through the strong pulses
in the hearts of my grandchildren
and they will not know when
they feel a snowdrop on their eyelid
it is their grandmother kissing them
again and again and again.
nor will they recognize me
in the eyes of a newborn
crying 'cause they have forgotten
that love once felt upon the earth
returns again and again and again
'cause nothing is ever lost.

*a*ll created phenomena rely on earth, fire, water, air and space in order to survive on earth. Otherwise there would be no stability and we would not be able to function. Gravity keeps us earthed but more than gravity is needed if we are to live, move and have our being-ness on the earth.

There are over twelve elements in our physical make-up and likewise many other energies such as electromagnetic, mechanical, chemical and bio-energetics that literally maintain us in human form, assisting us to function as such.

72% of our bodies consist of water and likewise the planet herself is manifested and mirrored in our physicality. This liquid element is found in the blood and other body secretions. 12% of our bodies make up the earth element: our bones and muscles keep the skeletal system together and earthed. 6% is air which finds manifestation in breath, whilst our bodily temperature is regulated by the fire energy which is 4% of body contents. Space, which is mostly recognized as a spiritual element, is indeed the consciousness in which we breathe. As soul is spaceless and timeless, when we die we leave this earth consciousness for another state of being in another life with other laws. But whilst grounded in earth the universal laws apply.

The visualizations provided in this chapter are done with dying people who have asked for help to leave the earth. They can also be experienced by those of us who are still strongly present on the earth. We just need to use our own wisdom and gauge whether or not they would be helpful for the dying person.

It is important to know beforehand the beliefs or spiritual precepts under which the dying person lived their life. This is not to say that the dying person may also change their minds about practices or prayers they might have normally relied on. Death often helps people to see through mists of misunderstanding around issues such as having a priest present to whom they may tell their sins. An elderly woman told me that she realized that she was not a sinner as she had been told, but that she was going to heaven "to be with Jesus, and he said nothing about me being a sinner. He just said come to me."

What Happens to the Cells?

When we are dying, something very special happens in our sacred physicality to support the soul leaving the body. The electro-magnetic energy centres in the body begin to lose their inner strength. I believe that this is when the light begins to dim in the cells of the body. Our full biological attention is given over to the dying process. When the light starts to diminish, the cell can no longer hold the energy and so deterioration begins. I was allowed to experience this dying process myself in meditation whilst still in good health.

As the life force leaves the body from the feet upwards, the light also leaves in this direction and so the trillions of cells in the whole body begin to sing the requiem for the form that is undergoing this transformation. The way I described this surreal experience was as if the sounding tones and hues from the exiting energy fields ascended, flowed into the music of the spheres back into formlessness and into consciousness again. This was for me, an extraordinary feeling, as if the physicality was also going through its own enlightenment. When the body dies and when the life force no longer supports the deteriorating cellular systems, the light goes out literally and the outer house is in darkness. The body is without the divine activator as the soul has returned to the great illumination.

During this Near Death Experience I was fully aware of each movement within my physiology, each impulse. Each tiny movement was felt to a heightened degree and as the lights were dimming in the centre of my cellular system I knew I was in control and could stop the process at any time using a certain kind of ujjayi breath, known as a sound or snoring breath, thus enlivening the form again. I believe that as the light travels through the body, leaving the body bereft of any voluntary movement, the heart still feels the magnificence of life force and continues supporting the soul in its last grand exit. The heart eventually also gives up the ghost or soul and bows to the angel of death. The Universal Heart then wraps the entity in deep, penetrating Love.

As the body's energy field or consciousness no longer has enough magnetism to hold onto the physical, to remain earthed, it moves in an anti-clockwise spiralling direction towards the top of the head, the crown chakra. Then the state of consciousness changes as the soul is now less earthed and we experience what we call "the tunnel experience". This is the place where, if there is unfinished business from the life just lived, we will review this life in the light of grace and non-judgment. It is the place of so-called darkness, as we have not yet fully ascended. At this stage we might not be able to take in the full electrical charge of light, as we may still be attached to ego mind where we experience the pain we inflicted on others. This stage is very short as we are still in transit to the illuminative light. The more we can keep our undivided attention on the light the more we will spiral upwards. If we have not been disciplined in our life journeys, we will be distracted very easily at this stage of our dying. But as light attracts light, and we no longer have the magnet energy to draw us or keep us attached to earth, or to the life just lived, we will be guided by the greater light.

A Physiology of Soul?

So, we name our physiology as the homing place of soul or life force as it imbues us and all creation with presence and movement. Maybe we can conclude that the soul has its being in the very nuclei, the very photons of light in the cellular structure of our human physicality. It is the spiritual DNA that lights up the whole of creation and us too.

May we learn to live Love so that the light can shine in the cells of our bodies and so lighten our own inner worlds of consciousness, infiltrate our biology and then affect the worlds of the collective.

> The egg of possibility
> Hatches in our readiness
> To bring our creative soul
> Into the soil of our ancestors
> Thus contributing to the telling of
> A brand new story
> Not only for our own next earthing
> But also for our children's children
> To the seventh generations.

The Earth Element Dissolves

Elisabeth Kübler-Ross described the grounding of life force as cathexing and the de-earthing of this life force as decathexing. This gradual dissolution of earth energy in the decathexing process is visible as it leaves form. Until I reached 70 years of age I did not notice any such phenomenon in my own body; I felt great energy for doing what I loved to do, ie., giving workshops and retreats in various places in Europe. Travel was not a problem, doing multiple acts simultaneously was not a problem. My schedule was quite filled but not stressed or hurried. Now however at 77, I find that the above activities have had to slow down as my inclination to be out there, active in the world, is desired less. It is not because I am no longer interested in the subjects I shared, rather it is because my dear body does not offer me the energy to do so. And this is natural. This is not about imminent death! This is about timing—knowing my own inner timing of things, listening to my soul and being led by the Universal Heart.

Thankfully I have trained others to go out there and do the work. Younger, more active women who just love to follow their souls' journeys as I do. This is also following the natural flow of nature; the older woman teaches the younger ones to share what they have learnt from the teachings and do it their own way, according to their beautiful intuitions and according to how grace expresses itself through them. This is about following the natural flow in nature.

Of course it is easy to notice how the earth energy begins to dissolve when a very ill person, whether older or younger, takes to their bed as gravity can no longer sustain them vertically on the earth. If we have learnt to listen to our own energetic rhythms when we were well and full of energy, we will appreciate when this energy is weak and we no longer have a desire to be active. Some may complain that they still want to do things and get frustrated when this is impossible. If we can surrender in the here and now to the timing of our souls, listen more within than without, it will be easier to tune into this energy when we are dying. Then we shall have no regrets or feel remorse when the time comes to surrender our earth energy with grace back into the earth again.

In the dying experience you may feel as if you are falling down through the bed and may think that you have disappeared into a cave of darkness. You may even feel that there is an earthquake and that the room is spiralling around. If you fear the dark at this moment this may prevent you from simply surrendering to the natural process. Here and now is the time to look at your fears of the darkness of the unknown.

When we hold too tightly to our possessions or to our families, they cannot truly be enjoyed, and this may hold us back when it is time to leave this world. During our lifetime it is good to practise setting free what is no longer available to us, whether that be our youth, a lover from the past or even a house; anything to which we hold tightly becomes a burden when we are dying. I feel that we never actually let anything go. It seems more natural to integrate all experiences, whether that be a memory of a loved one or the death of a sibling. Earth herself has a great hold on us while we are living on earth. This is good. The preservation of life is natural whilst still in the body. Some dear, dying people may go into deep guilt about the past and find it difficult to process it all.

When we can honour all experiences and integrate them lovingly; when death comes and they present themselves for our awareness—not judgment—we will smile on them like old friends now warmed at our hearts.

Sometimes you will notice the dying person will try and grasp the bedclothes very tightly. The physiology is assisting the will to stay on earth but natural weakness takes over. People grasp at material things for the last time, in the form of pressing themselves into the bed, or trying to hold on to the mattress or even grasping for a hand to hold on to. This is again the will trying to hold on to life. I have experienced this phenomenon with many dying people who were not ready to release their earth journey due to fear of the next life perceived to be hell. Here the earth element is the need to survive at all costs and still belong. And when the tired will feels that it no longer has a purpose, it panics. If this stage goes on for some time the breath also becomes panicky.

To prevent this stage from lasting too long in our own dying process, it is helpful to practise long out breaths, and pausing between breaths. It is also helpful to practise loving people and things, with no strings attached, to have deep compassion for each other and to be able to say "no". Knowing the timing of things; when to hold on and when to surrender naturally is a sacred practice in preparation for dying. The art of loving people and not using them as objects, sets them and us, free. The art of non-possessiveness of people and things not only frees us during life but supports us in surrendering earth life at death.

Many parents love their children and expect that they will be loved in return and that their children will be there for them when they are dying. This is distorted love. Children should not be used to take away our loneliness, to assuage a need for physical contact or to lessen our grief. We must learn to love them because they are beautiful expressions of life, and not beautiful expressions of us. We can learn to accept and give hugs and to touch things and people lightly so that in the end, we will be able to let go of the physical and material world and surrender to pure Love so that life may breathe in and through us with sheer joy.

ᕤ

A Blessing to Honour the Clay Body

Ah!
Red blood clay,
That fleshed these bones,
And gave softness to these joints!
Time now to cradle me, back until another spring.

How to Help the Dying Person

Often a dying person will feel that they are sinking into the ground and back into the earth. This is natural. Their helplessness will cause many to become depressed and hopeless, especially if they were very active in life and had not fully experienced everything they'd lived, owning and integrating those experiences or if there is unfinished business. Hold their hand if this is what they want and let them know softly, slowly that they are in their bed and all is well. I often have used the following words at this stage of the dying process with someone who loved the earth and was now leaving it:

I give thanks for all you did whilst you had strength to do it all.
I give thanks for the beautiful earth that you walked on
And the nature that you loved.
Now it is time to bring it all home in yourself.
Dear one, keep this image in your heart
You are not leaving anything
All is there within the inner fields of memory.

Integrating and Honouring the Outer

In the old days in Ireland, a dancer was invited to the room of the dying person whilst they could still be present and could converse. The family and the neighbours were invited to the "Last dance of the story" as the dancer who had known the dying person now danced their life back to them. This was to show them that they had lived a full life and could now, by the end of the dance, start freeing it. To assist the dying to do this, the dancer would slowly move downwards towards the earth in the last phase of the dance and lie there in peace for a while. I have done this sacred practice with many people and it was a joy both for the family and the dear one dying. There were also many laughs during the playback of the life as parts of the story might have been comical and all was expressed through the movements of Damhsa na marbh: The Dance of Death.

Visualization for the Watcher with the Dying

Imagine a deep terracotta colour.

See it, and feel it to be a clay texture, a mixture of deep orange, wine red with brown.

This is your first energy centre; feel comfortable in it.

You can even imagine yourself deep in it with your head above the earth.

Your eyes are closed.

Feel its warmth, feel its rich red earth colour in you.

Smell it—earth.

Sense it on your skin—earth.

Feel its warmth on your whole body—earth.

You are in it; it is in you. You love it.

You had times when you did not love it, but now you are so grateful for it.

It cradles you softly.

How it warms your heart and your being!

You know it so well and it holds you lovingly, and guards you. Here, right here, you are secure and nourished.

It is dark and smells of clay. Stay a while and sense the clay; the moist, dark, safe, earth clay all around you.

Now ever so slowly rise up from it. Wonderful strong arms help to lift you upwards.

Slowly feel your body moving away from the earth. You are being held, you are safe, you are loved.

Slowly up, up, up, out of the density. Feel the lightness of your body as you leave this dark red brown earth for another safe home.

Ah! Breathe in a short breath, and breathe out a long breath.

There is nothing in your hands, nothing to hold on to.

You are free, you are free, you are free.

Breathe in a short breath, breathe out a long breath.

Slowly rise up.

On the out-breath, say the words:

I rise up. I am free. I am free. I am free.
I rise up from and out of the earth.
I have nothing to hold, nothing to own, I need nothing now.
I feel only Love, only joy, only the deepest gratitude, now.

For us here and now still strong in our bodied selves, take a long breath in, hold for the count of 4, open your eyes and be still in body as you breathe out quickly through the mouth. Do this 4 times. Now move your body as it needs to be moved. This can be done alone but it is also so deeply memorable to do this with a friend or with a group.

This exercise has also been done with people outdoors, where participants actually bury themselves in the earth, horizontally and with the head free.

The Fire Element

Fire is the great cleanser, the great alchemist and a great primal element. It is awe-inspiring to realize that at death, the body supports all its internal functions and still intent on survival will fight against this alchemist, this transformer. The instinct to preserve life at all costs is well established in the human psyche since the beginning of time. But when we prepare ourselves and allow our bodies to get old and become feeble and we still have compassion and great love for it, it will just naturally surrender to the gentler call of death and enter the heart of dying without fear. There is often the struggle to stay here even when the time is right to leave. But when we realize the timing of our natures, the body will be free from the struggle.

The sacred alchemist called death burns what is not needed. Yin and yang are neutralized. Gender is also dissolved in the fire of transmutation of sexuality. Many times the dying person realizes the neutralization of their identity and becomes confused. As consciousness changes with the dissolution of the fire element, this message goes to the inner organs. Phosphor is emitted from the cells of the body, burns and finally extinguishes itself. Each photon of light is extinguished from the nuclei of the cells (about which process I have already spoken) and as the light leaves, the cells shut down. But remember the energy form of each organ remains, and the cells carry a trace memory into the ether.

I have noticed in my own body that the cleansing fire which is the great alchemist, is available for me here and now to transform old beliefs into healing truths. I often offer to the fire any inappropriate actions to do with the second energy field (the second chakra) such as inappropriate use of my sexuality when I was younger or feelings of arrogance that I harboured in my relationships. Physiologically, I also feel the ways in which the passion of blood through my body is less active than when I was younger. I notice the heat and the cold in my bones at various stages during the seasons. The fire energy is not as strong at the age of 77!

What Is Not Healed Revisits Us at Death

When Fire energy has all but left form, light photons from the weakened cells travel up the body and extinguish in each cell until they reach the head. Because of the accumulation of light the person may feel hot, then cold, then clammy as the temperature in the earth form fluctuates from fever to cold. Some people feel great frustration, and even irritation and annoyance. The nervous system it seems, is not equipped to deal with the intensely concentrated energy of fiery impulses throughout the system. As fire also represents electric charges, too much electricity can burn up the body too quickly. In life an overabundance of electricity in the body can lead to heart attacks, motor-neuron disease and conditions in which the nervous system is overwhelmed. The *anima* is undercharged or underfed and there is so much electrical energy in the system that it becomes overloaded. It's like revving the engine without pause. People who have been impatient and angry in life will feel the fire element rushing through the form. This is seen in the very red complexion of many dying people. The heart beats very fast with irregular beats and at times it may seem that it is not beating at all. The pulsating of the heart may sometimes be seen through the clothes of dying people like a panic impulse that almost shakes the form.

Relatives often share with me how a parent who had formally been very timid suddenly fights and pulls at them with anger and often curses and swears. This happens when the anger has been suppressed for years and suddenly revisits their psyches for healing. I tell the relatives that this is not about them, their parent has to go through their own inner struggles and that it is nothing they have done wrong. It is often difficult for us to see a parent suffering like this and all we can do to help is to not judge but to allow them to be with the pain whilst we hold them in our hearts with compassion for their struggle. If we suffer with them we cannot be of assistance. I said to a man whose father was showing signs of irritation, "Relax your breath, all is well. Go to your own room, light a candle. Sit and quieten your own breath. When you have done that, send a quiet breath to your father with the words, 'That anger is now being released from your past and all is well, you are safe.'" Within five minutes his father had quietened down and was alright again. We cannot help the dying if we get into the struggle with them. It is not our struggle but we make it so. We often behave likewise with the living. Let the Universal Heart hold all. We don't have to!

Metaphysically speaking at this stage of the dying process, the form is experiencing sensation as if the carcass is burning from within. In the Celtic expression we call it *Tine an tigh istigh* meaning "fire in the inner house". As fire is the only element that can defy gravity, it rises without any interference and without any resistance from the earth. This is also the time when dryness will appear on lips and skin. Thirst will begin to be apparent so to place little drops of water on the lips is helpful. The blood circulation will also be poor, so the lips and nails may appear purplish in colour. The arms, feet and legs will also take on a reddish purple colour.

୬

A Blessing to Honour Fire

Come fire,
Flame me back now
To your fiery embers
And smoke what needs renewing.
Oh! ancient alchemical symbol,
My faithful lover,
Come shape me to gold.

How to Help the Dying Person

Sometimes the dying person will feel like there is a fire in the room or even that there is molten lava present. Let them know in a whispered voice, or energetically, that this is not so. Sit quietly with the dying person, not touching them, as the body is now very sensitive to any outside pressure. Reassure them that the heat they feel is natural at this stage. All is well. They can just breathe gently although the breath may be drawn out and slow.

Any sexual inappropriateness suffered and not healed in the psyche can also arise at this stage for healing. As this can cause great shame and as the dying person is unable to understand what is taking place they may feel confused and afraid to die. I often add the sentence, "This too is forgiven", if the person was Christian. If self-compassion can be reached then this hell state of mind can be released into acceptance and eventually love. Encourage them to feel a sense of relaxation as they breathe out and relax into the openness of their own heart-fire always repeating the words, "Release, all is well." As I have already stated above, it is a good thing if you, as the carer for the dying person, have a small room of your own that you can return to, even a small space under the stairs where you can erect an altar with a candle and maybe incense and something like a stone or flower that means something to your heart, placed on it. Return every half hour to this blessed spot and renew your own energy by doing some strong breathing exercises, to renew your spirit when things get too much for you. Have some water nearby also. People tell me this can be a source of release for them when the watching with the dying goes on longer than they had anticipated.

Visualization

See the orange glow of fire burning all old beliefs about you.

The emotions that have not been felt can be released and can be set free.

Imagine the fire of love cleansing all the residue of past revenge and remorse.

You are being purified in the hot cauldron of love.
That which is not love is being burned away.
Fire is your dearest and most ancient, loving friend.
Breathe in slowly, a flow of silver.
Breathe out red orange fire of irritation and annoyance. Say:

The great alchemist, great life itself supports me. It burns whatever needs healing now, with my permission. I give myself, my ego-self, to this burning. I gladly offer the unhealed part of me, the conditioned self in me to the love of the universe. I return to what I am. I am love, I am love.

You can also add for yourself, *"I am love made visible in form."*

The Water Element and the Death Hormone

Water finally puts out the fire. The fire is then totally, and for this incarnation, extinguished. Water often symbolizes feelings that flow in and out of us. As all experience comes from inner projections, it is the mind that is producing these phenomena and not something from without. When the thinking is clear, the feelings can flow. When the mind is stirred, the feelings are also stirred. It often happens that someone who had appeared to have been very calm and introspective during their earthly life will suddenly become scared at this stage. If their calm has been a disguise for fear, the fear will look for release. How often I have encouraged my students to welcome in all feelings that are not comfortable, and fear is one of those feelings. Fear, like grief, jealousy, anger and so on, is searching for love, and unfortunately can cause great upset because we reject the feelings we don't like. They are like small children pulling at our clothes, looking our attention and will keep doing so until we become aware of them and welcome them all in. Only in the heart of compassion can our shadows feel safe and then may be released into Love.

Water is life giving and helps us to grow and mature whilst in form. It also acts as a conduit between us humans and the rest of creation. As we are decathexing from the earth we no longer need this element because life without form needs neither water, earth or fire, breath or space. When the oxygen is finally depleted in the brain, we release ourselves from time and space as these elements are also now unnecessary. The form itself now dries up and we return to dust or ashes and have no moisture. When the body dries up, the fluids in the muscles dry out so no further voluntary movement is possible. Urine may leak out of the body as the kidneys will have stopped working.

Do not worry if the urine is tea coloured as it will be very concentrated and has a deep, uncomfortable smell. Mucus may be emitted from the lungs and faeces may leak from the bowel. Beads of sweat may appear on the body and saliva may dribble from the mouth. We came from water and we return to the symbolic waters of life; the vast sea of awareness, consciousness. Contemplation on water and its cleansing nature can help us to release it when the time comes. Self-baptism is also a deeply cleansing sacrament which we ourselves can celebrate anytime. It renews us in the naming of ourselves as innocent, whilst on the earth and leaving it.

The Death Hormone

The pineal gland lies at the centre between the two brain hemispheres and is mostly known for its influence on melatonin and pinoline. It is situated at that place where Jewish men wear the yarmulke and the Pope wears the pileolus. Descartes called the pineal gland "the seat of the soul". In the Celtic tradition it was named "the house of Love" and Hindu monk Swami Vivekananda, referred to it as "the shining light of God's grace, between the portals of thought". As the water element is dissolving the pineal gland opens with the breath and a hormone called DMT is released in large amounts into the bloodstream. Dr Rick Strassman calls DMT "the death hormone" since it opens the being into joy, inner sight and inner hearing. This hormone acts as a means of slowing down the breath so that the space between breaths is longer and a deep, peaceful calm is experienced by the dying person. *Ayahuasca*, a mood-changing traditional medicine used by shamans of indigenous countries also contains the death hormone. It is said to transport one into different internal states of consciousness. If the soul is at peace, they say the experience will be harmonious, but if the soul is not at peace, the inner journey could be tumultuous (the heaven/hell belief system).

A Blessing to Honour Water

Dried up on this ashen floor
Water all sucked back to sea
I creep back to the womb of grace
Small boat floats upon the shore.

How to Help the Dying Person

If the dying person acts as if they are drowning or suffocating and taking great gulps of air, help them by whispering soft words of comfort or speaking to them energetically. Let them know they are lying in bed and that all is well. As consciousness will be expanding at this stage, very gently place your hand near theirs but not on it. They will feel your comfort without you having to touch them. Let them have some moisture on a sponge to help relieve dryness in the mouth and throat. I usually whisper my name and say, "This is Phyllida, whom you know. I am dampening your lips. All is well."

At this stage of dying, all the energies of the dying person will be directed at the inner journey. The "death hormone", like the birth hormones, will soon relieve them of any pain and will result in bringing inner freedom and the inflow of joy.

As the dying are no longer interested in the outer world, at this stage, many will experience that their dead relatives are there to meet them. (This has been revealed in Near Death Experiences.) Often the dying will sit up in the bed unaided, and look ahead as if at a scene before them. My own mother exclaimed as she reached this stage of her dying process, "I see the mother of Jesus and she is smiling at me. Ahh, mother!" I noticed my mother's smile was heavenly as she was nearing the end of her earth life. She looked so young and wrinkle free. Soul had penetrated her whole being and the dear old ego had been wrapped in the love of her God.

The sense of hearing is still operating at this stage so it is important to have peace in the room. As the bliss hormone travels slowly through the remaining energy centres, heaven is experienced by many. Physiologically, the body is clammy and the nose seems to be deflated as the breath labours in the chest. At an emotional level, the dying person is no longer attached to family or people around them. Their minds are travelling on, following their thought projections. Spiritually they are opening up more and more to their "Godselves". They are going home to the centre of themselves at last, and will soon have no more earth experiences this time.

Visualization

Think of and visualize water.

Imagine you are deep in the warm waters of the sea.

Now, see yourself walking out of the sea.

Feel the water on your body.

Feel your hair drip with water.

Feel it on your face.

Feel it clear your mind of all distractions.

There is no wind blowing, just the sun shining on and in the water and on your body.

Sit down.

Feel the sand under you, absorb the water and feel the sun dry each single drop.

Look out to the sea again. It is vast, unending and still.

Open up to the heartbeat of the ocean and feel at one again, again, again with water.

Give thanks for your own purification in the vast waters of life. Feel yourself as vast and strong as the waters of the Atlantic.

Drink it in with your mouth and then breathe out.

Let go into the ocean, let her take your body discomforts into the sea of life itself.

Feel the clear blue stream of consciousness flow throughout your entire being like a soft, gentle wave. Say:

I am being cleansed in the vast sea of grace.
My whole being is being transformed into the fluidity of the oceans. I open to a more expanded life, to the vast sea of life. I let the waters heal my thoughts and mind of all unhelpful visions. I open my mind to the joy that was always there. It fills me. Joy widens my heart, dancing it into the heart of the universe. Life lives me now, fully.

Take time to lie still and feel the waters of the vast sea of divine consciousness release your joy.

Breathe in now.

Breathe out now.

Breathe in "thank you".

Breathe out "thank you".

Take your time before you rise up and raise your arms to the sky in gratitude.

The Air Element

It is time now to leave the earth plane behind. As the last out-breath carries us out of the earth, it does so slowly and consciously. Nothing is done in haste. Each process has its own rhythm and timing. Death does not happen suddenly, not even in sudden death. Each sacred expression is carried out with an orderly and pulsating sequence. Like the energy rhythms of the chakra systems each stage takes its time to flow into and merge with the one that went before, and in this vibrational dance of emergence we are again and again reminded that as in the beginning, so in the end. Just as the birthing process is not over and done with when the child is born, other important stages have to be orchestrated before completion. Had we the eyes to see and the ears to hear we would be truly astounded at the activity taking place biologically and energetically within the transforming body/mind.

In my own NDE (Near Death Experience) in 1973 I remembered travelling out of form and observing or witnessing phenomena happening from another viewpoint. I could actually see that my two-year-old daughter was safe in a neighbouring house and that the doctor wore a lovely coloured tie. I wondered why the priest kept insisting that my sins were forgiven because from this neutral viewpoint I didn't have sins! I remember smiling at his naivety! Later after I "came back from the dead" the same priest said that I would have died a very happy death as I looked angelic. Little did he know why I was smiling!

When the death has happened and the person is announced clinically dead—brain dead—we believe that's it now, she's gone to heaven. This is a simple way to view the dying process. Whilst the dear form cannot resurrect as there is now no life force to animate it, soul is about to experience many more passageways before it reaches unity consciousness—the internal, holy marriage, the *Hieros Gamos* in Greek. Life force is returned to the dimension of spirit.

In this material dimension we live in day by day, we see only in part. Because we concentrate on the world of form more than on the world of spirit it is as if we see dimly through a glass. We hear only with the physical ears and feel only with the emotional heart. When we release our last breath, we have the possibility, according to our spiritual evolution, of moving into other dimensions. This is facilitated by a strong spiritual electrical impulse. We know intuitively that this is not the end, this is but a rite of passage to another existence, no less real than the one we have exited from.

According to Dr Nancy Evans Bush, the hormone DMT propels us further and further from earth and it is often called the "spirit molecule". However if we are still attached to ego dimensions within ourselves, we will still be somewhat magnetized to earth properties. The laws of gravity may still maintain a hold on our astral body and keep it earthed, if it has not resonated with soul during its earth time. This is not a judgement, just a fact. Many are not interested in things of the spirit and have more resonance with the material. Maybe their time for soulful living was not on their agenda this time round. But it will happen eventually and soul does not live in time and space so, all is well and in accordance with the neutral laws of spirit.

The astral body referred to above, has no density of its own, rather it is the emotional patterns and thought patterns belonging to the personality that housed it. It can travel through density as it is disembodied. If at any time this entity which may have remained on earth after the departure of soul wishes for release, it can draw on the help of higher, evolved beings to assist it to leave the earth plane and travel via electric impulse to the light, its source. We can also help these entities to leave the earth plane by our rituals of releasing. These rituals are all important and I have initiated many of them.

As I stated before, the astral body consists of all our emotional experiences and belief systems. At death, that which is healed, no longer draws us to earth experiences as its resonance is with soul and soul travels to its source, spirit. The soul always travels home after death of form. When this is our reality we can say along with Jesus the Christ, "It is finished."

A healed life form will leave behind it an emanation or vibrant energy of quiet peace and joy, whilst the unhealed form leaves behind an energy of disquiet. Emotions are energy-filled entities and remain in the astral realm. The unhealed shadowed self may attach itself to members of the family or friends who carry the same or similar difficult life experiences, such as alcoholism and other addictions that keep the astral body close to earth. If the emotional heart has not transformed into the Universal Heart, then unhealed emotions will still create problems. Often if the dead person had unfinished work to do, for example if they left the earth not having met a debt or left with a secret that affects the family, they may try to reach a family member that they had been close to and appear to them in the dream time to try and put things right. Unfortunately this does not always work and family feuds can ensue.

Each of us, with the help of spirit guides, has prepared for ourselves our next life experiences. As above, so below. There is a particular energy field to fit all stages of spiritual development. We will enter into the one best suited to our own spiritual journey after death and before conception. "In my father's house there are many mansions."

No one demands or pronounces your place in your next life experience, and again I repeat, no God sits in judgement of your last incarnation. Ultimately, your own free, healed will, together with your soul guide, decides how you will progress spiritually. You will have had many chances to transform the personality. If you had chances and did not avail of them, this means that you will experience similar situations again that will help you to respond, rather than react on your next journey to heal further. Life and Love are neutral energies of consciousness; they are incapable of judgement or retribution.

They are not capable of punishing you, as they do not possess a personality.

When the breath becomes laboured in the dying process, the person may experience a sense of being closed in. They may try to maintain control by struggling to breathe when the breath is longing to be released. This leads to confusion as oxygen is still travelling to the brain. Whilst this happens they can have various fluctuating thinking processes and they are often hazy and confused. This also occurs when one is in a coma. Past experiences of being suffocated or strangled may visit us and panic may ensue.

Breathing is symbolic of taking in and letting go. It is about coming and going and it also represents the personal and the collective. If the person has learned to surrender to life, the last breaths will be gentle. The out-breath will be long and relaxed and there will be no panic when the breath stays out a long time. When there seems to be a long time between out-breath and in-breath, a sense of joy will flow in, as the dying one sinks into total surrender and peace.

At this stage there will be release from all earthly involvement. The physical, emotional, and intellectual quadrants will have all been shut down gradually and the being will open wide into the light of divine grace, and become consumed by it. This process of withdrawing from earth life is often reflected in the lack of interest in the world around them, even a sense of disconnecting from the family and cares of the family. Time will be blurred and often I have noticed many times how the dying person, whilst still conscious will ask many times what time it is. They seem to float between worlds and the idea of time becomes confusing. My father asked one day, "Is it night time yet, because it seems very dark?" When my brother answered that it was 2 o'clock in the afternoon he looked puzzled. Later on he no longer asked this question.

From a scientific perspective when there is no longer a supply of oxygen to the brain, the higher cortex opens and one experiences the light photons that exist in this part of the brain. It will seem like an explosion of various coloured lights. Whilst this is a beautiful experience, it is a distraction which the mind permits at this stage. Discipline is required to go towards the pure radiance, rather than stop off at the fireworks display! People who meditate are more disciplined mindfully and know that this rainbow of delight is not the pure light of Love. However some beings may decide to stay in this place for a time and savour the joy.

We aim to have self-discipline, to become a disciple of the self or soul so that we may surrender further and deeper into pure consciousness. We at last unite with pure Love and this is indeed the place of no return; *ait gleagail an grá* meaning "the rapture place of Love".

ⳤ

A Blessing to Honour Air

Breath now leads me to silence,
No longer one with the story.
Now beyond the telling,
It returns to mystery.

How to Help the Dying Person

The dying person, if not prepared to release the last breath, may feel suffocated. I remember sitting by a dying person and breathing very softly and gently beside the bed. I allowed my breath to remain outside my body for as long as it was comfortable. Then I would whisper,

> All is well, surrender to the breath.
> You do not have to struggle to breathe in again.

Let the breaths go.
You are safe.
Follow the silver light.
Fall into the light.
Release the breath, release the breath,
release the breath into the light.

This I would do three or four times until the patient was relaxed and not panicking. This *anal marbhu* meaning "death breath" can be practised during the day by those of us who are still living. The ancient Yoginis practise it and it is called "Prana Kala". Kala was the god of death and he was called upon to lead the last breath to the light. In Ireland it was said that Brigid herself stood by the bedside of the dying and showed them how to breathe gently. At last she would breathe out on them and they would simply let go with a sigh and be released into the arms of Love.

Visualization

A silver hue is being breathed into your internal organs via the bindu energy centre at the back of the head and then out into the Universe via the solar plexus.

Imagine you are dying and your breath is gentle and easy. Keep it very gentle and easy throughout this practice.

See the family sitting around.

Their grieving is done.

Only a sense of release pervades the room.

All is well.

This life form has surrendered itself into Love.

You breathe out fully now into your own dying moment.

You are safe.

Say:

> *I am breath, I come, and I go.*
> *Breath comes, breath goes.*
> *I take life in. I integrate life.*
> *I am consciously alive in breath.*

Then take a deep breath to the count of four, hold it for the count of six and release it to the count of eight. Take time to come back, fully alive, breathing gently and ready for the next movement.

Space

What is space? As we live in time and space it is not possible for us to imagine spacelessness. Perhaps space could be seen as a vast, expansive dimension of consciousness that is used by consciousness to provide a container for our earth experiences. It can also be explained as the presence of pure neutrality, or detached Love, which contains life itself in form creating harmony and balance. Imagine that space contains mystery and at the centre of that mystery, consciousness dwells.

Our spirit home is spacelessness and timelessness. We are going home into the mystery again, into consciousness. Although confined to time in the here and now, space, together with time, provides us with a matrix in which we can experience earth life. Space on its own is timeless. Time and space belong with form, and space in its natural state is as free as the soul when it is freed from earthly confinement. If we learn to be more conscious of the space around and about us we will realize that there is no such thing as nothingness. Even in the so-called emptiness of space, consciousness is moving continuously, creating from thought and continuously re-creating from the ashes of our past.

At death, we emerge from space and time into spacelessness and timelessness. In the meantime however we live confined to the limitations of form and the material. Having breathed our last out-breath we simply travel in spacelessness which provides the soul with the next energy field wherein it can experience further life, in what is called "Aíte" (Gaelic) or "Bardos" (Tibetan), until the next chosen form is taken.

> Nothing is ever lost
> All is gathered in at last.
> With every being that leaves
> I leave in them.

ᎣᏍ

A Blessing to Honour Space

This is not my first time journeying here.
I have taken this route
From timelessness to time-fullness
To re form
To re deem
To re dress
To re do
All that went before
Time and time again and again and again
Into space, the sacred womb of experience.

How to Help the Dying Person

Say into the right ear of the dying person *(Do not stand too close):*

> "All is well
> nothing can draw you back now
> keep travelling on in joy
> until your soul reaches home."

Visualization

Sit on a chair or lie on the floor.
  Close your eyes on the world of distractions.
  Breathe gently, slowly, very quietly and evenly.
  Say the words slowly and with intent.

  I am quiet now, drifting into the vastness of the sky.

Sense yourself drifting in timelessness and in spacelessness.
  Feel it, feel a sense of not having a body. You are a no-body.
  And feel a sense of being without a past. Without a future.
  You are without a dream, without regret, without a goal.
  Have the awareness—I am space-less, I am time-less.
  I am.
  Breathe gently and after some time, breathe deeper, into
the lower body. Sound the breath throughout your body with
a sigh... Ahhhh!
  Say, looking out the window or into a mirror (translated
from old Gaelic):

> *Nothing can hold me down,*
> *Nothing can draw me up,*
> *Nothing can take me under,*
> *No false light can attract,*
> *No false song can seduce.*
> *No memory can bind me,*
> *No earth love can find me,*
> *I am no longer lost,*
> *I am no longer found,*
> *I am no longer me and us and them.*
> *I am and I am not.*

What are you feeling after this slow practice?

Psycho-Spiritual Pain at Death

Medical staff in hospices are learning more and more about non-physical suffering as death draws near. Emotional suffering can be painful for a dear one who suddenly remembers acts of inappropriateness or similar, and when there is no witness to this pain they can die carrying this to their next experience of life, thus preventing full joyful dying and much confusion after death. I used to sit with such dear people and just say the words, especially to those of a Christian background: "That too is forgiven. Can you too forgive yourself? No one is judging you now." Remember that the brain is not yet dead so it is still recording and the old memories are present and old regrets can cause us suffering even at the last breath. Now is the time to think consciously, and therefore live more responsibly day by day, so that our dying may be glorious and joyful for us and all beings. Today is the day when you forgive yourself. Do not wait for your dying day. With self-compassion you will see that there is no need for forgiveness as far as your soul is concerned. It is the judgments of your earth mind that create the inappropriate guilt that leads to self-condemnation. It is so important dear one, to create a loving, compassionate relationship with your own heart. Have a strong love affair with it.

Create a pure relationship in which sad and often shameful stories from the past may be exchanged in an atmosphere of mutual respect and deep acceptance. Imagine being able to hold your own heart and feel the cloak of the Universal Heart softly cradling you both in the most exquisite safety of love. Can you imagine your heart at death and all that it had to hold inside? When it beats for the last time can you say, "Thank you for accepting and loving me throughout the years"? Why not begin this practice today? Get to know the rhythm of your own heartbeat, feel it strong in you and with deep gratitude thank it for its devotion to your life. When the end of its work is done, it can release itself into the ether with joy and gladness overflowing with love for you who cared for it whilst it was beating and drumming in you.

"The great adventure," as Alice Bailey calls death, happens when the heart flatlines, sings its last hallelujah and there are no more vital signs left in the form. But that is not the end, as we well know. Now the real story can take place, the adventure of the soul after it has been freed. Earth life for this being has come to an end and another mystery is about to begin—an inner mystery filled no less with passion, adventure, experiences, curiosities, beauty, self-doubt, insecurities, shadowlands and so on. You see, as below so above, as above so below. The kaleidoscope of life keeps this universal law in movement.

The Soft Morning … from the Gaelic

The love that called you
Will recall you
When the soft morning comes.
The breath that breathed you
Will release you
When the soft morning comes.
The light that brightened you
Will enlighten you
When the soft morning comes.

The Dissolution of the Material Body

What happens to the atoms that are released from the molecules when they are dispersed from the electromagnetic structure of form? Do they re-form, rebuild themselves into other molecular processes in the ether and create other life forms? It is well established that our thought patterns created form in the beginning, and as in the beginning, so in the end. The Celtic tradition supports the belief that nothing is lost or forgotten in the story of creation. Molecules that resulted from old thought patterns fuse with molecules resulting from new thought patterns to create a new being on earth. This is known as *corpa bailighaigh* meaning "gathered in body". It is reasonable to suggest that nothing actually dies at death, not even the elements which constitute the body and so a continuation of a life continues.

What happens to the encoded messages within these new, focused molecules? Science tells us through the theory of entanglement that particles once joined cannot separate, meaning that even when they are separated they behave as if they are still together. In other words, we can say that our form, after death, does not fully disintegrate and is forever connected energetically to creation. All life is energy. All thought is energy, and is always creating and always in movement towards unity consciousness. There is no separation even at death. This poses the question of the quality of energy we will leave behind us on earth when our soul travels to its source. I have had the awesome experience of being able to see with my physical eyes an energy entity that hung around a dead person for some time after the soul had departed. The personality belonging to that particular soul was steeped in drug abuse and alcohol before they died. Above his head was a cloud of dark grey matter floating just by the ceiling. I spoke to it with my imagination. Taking full internal authority, I said the words:

"Dear one, go to the place you have prepared for yourself because and on account of your choices in life. You chose to abuse your body/mind which were not yours to misuse. There is a place reserved for you. Go with the intention of healing this time and ask for the help to do so. Go in peace and in compassion."

It might sound rather self-flattering to add that when I had spoken the words the grey cloud disappeared. I have experienced this phenomenon many times with dying people who had not considered changing destructive habits and addictions before death. When one watches a lot with dying people, one's extrasensory perception grows. This has been my experience.

As a healing force death has the potential to free families into great healing. Sometimes family feuds are settled and people once at war with one another may suddenly start speaking to each other and forgiving one another. Death can also be a time of great healing for the dying person as they have time to reflect on the past life and make amends. I also oftentimes witnessed death as an act of great love as the body offers itself to the soul. The soul needs to free itself from the confines of matter when its time has come. This is difficult to comprehend when a child or young person dies. We say it is not fair. But we do not know the timing of each soul. Having lived a short time in earth life might be exactly why the soul took form, just to taste human connection, human space and time. Therefore, seeing as love is about harmony and balance, what we have not healed in this body form or what is left unfinished in one lifetime will always seek homoeostasis and more completion in the next incarnation.

Look at your body now and look at a photo of your body taken ten years ago. So much has changed in you physically as well as psychologically and energetically in the intervening time. To age is natural, to mature intellectually is natural and to evolve spiritually is of course also natural. Each new experience in life provides us with more so-called grist for the mill of the ageing process. My grandchild loves to examine my face and remind me "There is no more elastic in your face Granny P, you need some good creams." Only the innocence and honesty of a child could speak such truth!

We have to remember that the inner processes of our minds are also living organisms and change with the altering states of awareness and forgetfulness we move through during the day. Stress shape-changes the physical and likewise alters the thought processes. Age affects the cells in the physical body as well as the flexibility of cells in our higher cortex. As human beings we live on a spectrum of loving life and living it fully, or being afraid of life and refusing experiences out of fear. We need to nourish our minds with conscious awareness of the thoughts that we indulge in as they are creating our outer experiences all day long.

It is possible though, to change our beliefs in response to our experiences, and thus to increase our inner wisdom. I define wisdom for me as "knowledge derived from healed experiences". This is a means to enlightenment while still in the body. My sense is that if we can accept the ageing process as a natural state of being human without striving to stay forever young, we can gently and easily also release any thoughts of jealousy, bitterness or arrogance that have been building up during the years. It is sad to see an embittered old person, not willing to release others from blame or self from inappropriate guilt. The defensive walls we have built around our lives are not easy to tear down once we reach our dying stage.

Many live lives in agony longing for the good old days, but they cannot be relived. This is a very depressing place for an older person to live in. An un-lived life has only memories to bring comfort, memories and a melancholy, longing for things to be different.

If we have not learnt to release blame and judgments during earth life, it is not easy to die in peace and harmony with the world. I remember the old Irish saying,

> Na beidh ag fanacht
> Go la na stoirme
> Go gcoirigh tu an dion.

Meaning…do not wait until the day of the storm before you fix the roof!

Soul Release Blessing

This is a Celtic method for helping the soul or life force to release without hindrance. The releasing words must be handed down verbally. This practice is similar to the one described by Ramana Maharishi, the Indian sage. After his mother passed away in 1922, Ramana writes:

As I sat with my left hand on her head, my right hand on the heart, innate tendencies became very active. Scene after scene rolled before her in subtle consciousness. As the outer senses had already gone, the ego went through a series of experiences that may have required many more births of her. But the quickening process worked by the special touch given to her on this occasion, means the soul was at last disrobed of its subtle sheaths before it reached the final destination. The supreme peace from which there is no return to ignorance.

There is a practice, which has been requested by dying people, when they could communicate with me before they entered into the dying phase. This practice can sometimes last for over half an hour so deep compassion, deep presence and patience are absolutely necessary. Of course the family will have been told of this practice so no one is feeling awkward. The dying person decides whether the family members stay in the room during the practice or vacate it. It is their decision always.

Our gentle non-judgmental presence will act as a sweet balm to the whole life and death experience of the departing or departed soul. When I sense that the blessing is complete, I wait for a while in presence and give great gratitude for the sacred beings that have assisted me throughout. Sometimes despite the fact that I would have discussed the practice with the dying person whilst they were still connecting with me verbally, it can happen that at the actual time of dying you may feel it is not appropriate. You have to listen to your own intuition. Here is the method I have used:

The Sacred Practice

With watchful presence and total focus I very, very lightly hover my left hand around the top of the head of the dying person with my right hand hovering over the heart.

I sit for a while contemplating these two blessed sites in the body imagining them opening into the internal vibrations and energy fields.

Then I gently withdraw the right hand, and with spiralling right hand movement, draw the light of life force from the feet, through the energy centres to this spot, whilst repeating certain blessings of release.

As I draw what I perceive as the dark grey colours that represent unfinished energy in the various energy centres gently upwards towards the head, I wait and watch with the personality as it still tries to control. I may say the words, *"It is safe to release all struggle now."* I may repeat these words or similar comforting words during the practice.

At a certain stage some time later, when I realize that life force is gently flowing throughout the form and breath is waiting to be released, I slowly release the practice and always finish by drawing my hands together at the top of the head and so release any stuck energy. I then wash my hands in a small basin of cold water when I am finished. (The basin of water I would have placed on a chair before I'd have begun the practice.)

I then very slowly withdraw my energy from the bed, leave the room and call the nurse as I know death is imminent. When it was a home death, I always took note of time of death as this is important to family members who would have noted the time had they been in the room, but might for instance, have been in the kitchen. It is quite a journey for breath to take and often one will think the person has died when suddenly they begin breathing again. Often the heart carries on beating and again it takes time for it too to stop the drumming and be in the peace of Love. As I have written before, dying can be a slow experience for many. Each stage has to be gone through and completed before the next stage begins. (Of course this is not so in sudden death or accident.)

Philosophy on the Phenomenon of Dying

As we know, life force or consciousness is present in all form and vitalizes or animates it. Scientific investigation shows this to be evident even in the smallest particle of matter. Thus, the source from which all matter is birthed cannot change and cannot die. It is formless. As this source constitutes the very essence of our being as humans, this aspect in us and of us never ceases to be. It goes on to live and experience, grow and mature spiritually in another sphere, the sphere of Spirit. It is always evident to me and to those who have watched with the dying, when the soul departs the form. The energy in the room changes dramatically and a felt sense of void remains. A sense of lifelessness. The animation which vivified the form has departed and left behind the shell which housed the beloved. The dear shell is no longer capable of housing this awe-full, immense energy. It will have its own resting place back in the earth again. Ashes to ashes, dust to dust.

> Oh happy joy-filled dancing one
> savour this time with your beloved
> for sure as he delights your heart
> with Summer kisses and winter white
> so will he cast your form aside
> as death reshapes you
> back to its earthen clay
> no longer fit to serve the dance.

The potential of a new form of life is already present in all forms of life. In order for that potential other life to emerge, the old one has to let go and allow the new to evolve. This time of transformation is what we call "death". The chrysalis has to let go of its form so that the butterfly, already within the pupa, can emerge. Thus death is very present in life and life is also present in death. The one holds the key of evolution to the other. "For sure as he delights your heart, so will he cast you from his side." These words sound harsh and unloving yet, death like life, is neutral. We have to somehow humanize it, give it a personality in order to try and understand the mystery.

To live this paradox is to live in the now, always allowing what needs to transform in and around us to do so. After we die to our body, the dancer will come again if we have not completed our dance—that is all the things we wanted to do in life. We will return to do these things, to dance them. The dance must be completed no matter how short or how long it takes. When we have experienced all that we had chosen to live, we will not come here again. All will have been stirred back into Love.

But that will not be the end, as we have already said life force cannot suffer annihilation. We will surely continue to express life force in another sphere, in a spiritual and unformed way. It all has to do with our own integral spiritual evolution which may be experienced here or in parallel lifetimes or in another dimension.

It is an amazing gift to experience life in human form, here and now with other life forms. When we let go of this form, a truly magnificent process takes place. Birth to form and death from form are natural processes, but generally we do not retain the memory of our birth and of our previous death. As we become more conscious we will see that all life is happening simultaneously in the "now" of our experience. I am both coming and leaving all in one breath as soul is timeless. For me it is so mysterious and awe-inspiring to know that I am already enlightened. And my dear personality, my earth mind neediness has to go through the process, and it is slow. It just needs time!

Imagine if we could truly see how the whole of life, all our incarnations from the very first to the last is but an in-breath coming into form and an out-breath going out of form and the pauses in-between are the experiences we have as we express life.

Where are the borders of time? When do the moments that we understand as time start and where do they end? With increasingly precise scientific measurement of unbelievably small amounts of time we begin to see that eternity is present in the moment of now.

When this life force needs to leave human form, unless we have had an accident or an illness, old age is the natural way for it to leave. In many of the old traditions, old people lived longer as they lived closer to nature, and were more in tune with themselves and all other beings. They were aware of when the time to leave their form was approaching and advised the family to organize the rituals for dying. Nowadays, many people have lost the intuitive ability to know when death is near. I believe as I am the author of my birth so am I also the determiner of my hour of death. In an out-of-body experience I was shown the date of my death this time. Just as well this book is getting written now!

We have lost the natural gift of tuning into our own inner wisdom and finding answers there. When we reach a deeper knowledge of what the dying process really is, we will know that life cannot die, therefore neither can we, or rather the *what* of me will never endure death. And when the *what* of me has fully in-bodied the *who* of me, then I will have been infused with the love of the Universal Heart which is true unemotional compassion. Ahh! Moment of ecstasy!

Then the dancer, the dance and the completion of this dance will have bowed down to life—the initiator of the dance and also the reason for it!

The Astral Body

There are many ways to describe the astral body and I have chosen to describe it in the way I experienced it during both my NDE and through my own intuitive inner knowing. Deep in trance during a self-induced shamanic healing it was through a felt sense that I experienced the extension of my own auric or energy fields. I imagine people from other traditions might refer to a different model whilst defining astral body. My belief is that our astral bodies are replicas or templates of our physical bodies which have been formed through the process of our own electromagnetic energetic systems of which I wrote about earlier. They emit an energetic aura which some people, including myself are able to see. When the elements have left the form, there is still the astral body left in the EMF but when the ego and soul have become integrated, the astral body no longer remains. It aligns with soul and travels with it to source. I imagine that is what is known in the Catholic faith as Assumption when Mary the mother of Jesus was said to be "assumed into heaven, body and soul".

This transparent non-material body known as astral does not have inner, dense organs and cannot communicate except from mind to mind. It does not have substance but is the energetic membrane which informs our senses, instincts and emotions. Our astral bodies sense the world around us through the energetic connection that brings the information to the heart. When the heart is open and we are living congruently with the world, our inner fields of energy shine outwardly and extend quite a distance from the physical body.

The astral body, when no longer attached to the physical body, can walk through doors, appear to people, and can even seem to communicate telepathically. These beings are known as ghosts. If the ego energy of a dead relative has been healed at source, an emanation or light body may appear to the family assuring them that all is well. This is not the person as they were, rather it is the energetic body which can impress itself upon the mind of another. This can be an act of service of love to the relative, as the emanation has to lower its vibrations and frequencies in order to enter the density of earth life.

An astral body may become earth-bound when it does not realize that the body is dead as in the trauma of sudden death or has not yet adjusted to this fact. When it does adjust, and is in a state of grace and Love it may join the life force and go to source. But the astral body is no wiser than the last state of the mind and emotions of the person who died. Just because someone is dead does not mean that they are any wiser than when they were alive on earth. The astral body is not the same as the ethereal body which comprises pure ether or consciousness and returns to source. It does not rely on form for its energetic life. I like to describe soul as the messenger of spirit.

At this time in our world we are all traumatized in one way or another by the pandemic called Covid-19, a Coronavirus. Many are leaving the earth in great fear and many of those are in hospitals, feeling they are alone and forgotten as they lie in isolation, scared of dying. It is therefore absolutely imperative that we who are well can offer rituals of healing compassion for these dear people.

Imagine the astral bodies that are at present roaming our earth totally confused and in a state of fear, not knowing what is happening. They possibly know they have passed over to a new dimension but more than likely they had been unconscious for a long time, in a state of half-life, half-death, and heavily drugged. This fear still haunts the earth and we are all somehow soaking it up, especially people who resonate with it, those who already carry fear in their own consciousness.

I have done many rituals of releasing such beings into the compassionate arms of love where fear can rest and these dear beings may rest in peace at last. It seems right that we all perform these rituals in order to clear our own psyches of the remnants of fear and trauma.

One cannot connect with the soul of another because their frequencies, vibrations and their spiritual energy is too strong and too light-filled. Therefore it is up to the light energy of the soul to connect with earth, not the other way around. I believe that the energy left behind by a light-filled person or being contributes and helps to heal those on earth. Many people who pass on, bless earth with their love or ethereal energy and grieving persons have also been comforted by this.

Perhaps in the future, if the vibrational rate of humanity increases, it may become more commonplace to be able to connect with the dying or those who have passed over. But the permission has to be there as it is not a right we have to enter the spirit world merely because we would like to.

For someone who has experienced a trauma accompanied by a Near Death Experience, it may be difficult for them to integrate this into their everyday awareness. The longing for the beloved self that they may have glimpsed in the other realm, or the other world within, may prevent them from living in the here and now within the confines of the body. They may have enjoyed the out-of-body experience so much that they have problems in lowering their vibrations again to come back into the body. The trauma affecting the nervous system in an accident, facilitates the astral body to leave the broken body and the site of the accident. Many people suffer deep depression when they return to their bodies having had this experience and cannot often find the words to relate the experience to others.

When I experienced my own NDE in 1973 in Northern Ireland where I was living at the time, I found it very difficult to return to the body-life again.

As I have shared before, my astral body did travel and was able to perceive my child being cared for although I was in hospital some miles away. The peace and astute awareness I experienced was so amazing. In the end it was the crying of my husband that brought me back to body-life. I knew I had to return, and that saddened me quite a lot. In this altered state I was not emotionally involved with my daughter at all and this quite surprised me as we were inseparable otherwise.

Many people refer to the soul leaving the body during an NDE but this is not really the case. When the soul leaves the body, one dies. The life force or silver cord detaches. The astral body however can leave any time, especially at night during dream time.

Questions to Explore

- What is life?
- What is death?
- Are you faithful to yourself?
- Are you faithful to life?
- What are your fears of life?
- What are your fears of death?
- What are your experiences of someone dying?
- What are your beliefs about an afterlife?
- What would you like to believe?
- Why not believe this?
- How free are you to choose?
- Which beliefs from your ancestors do you believe?
- Do they serve you?
- Do they serve the community?
- Do you believe you have the right to change your beliefs?
- What are your fears about changing your beliefs today?
- Investigate the idea "I will live forever" or the continuity of life.

Chapter 111

Healing the Family Tree

Ancestral Healing

They're coming
They're coming out of the past
Passing through you
Passing through me and all of us
Often I feel their breath
Disturb my heart beat
And humbled by
Their need, now mine
I sink beneath their burden
And watch the too slow caravan
Stumble miles and miles of
Dried-out bones
Crushed from the sorrowing
I break in pieces
Yet on they slowly march
Seven sorrows deep
Until at last I barter back
These pieces of the cross
For seven gifts
And they undone till now
Do bow in gratitude
Burst through
And leap with surer step
And dance the living and the dead
In love.

Life sends us forward with some thing(s)
unhealed from the past.
– Mark Wolynn, *It Didn't Start with You*

The most powerful ties are the ones to our parents.
It does not matter how many years have passed, how many
betrayals there have been, how much misery in the family,
we remain connected even against our wills.
– Anthony Brandt, "Bloodlines", *Esquire*

☙

The traumas experienced by our ancestors; their griefs un-grieved, their lives not lived, their broken-heartedness not mended, their fear of poverty never ended and their dreams for a better tomorrow never reached, all affect us at some level. Your own nervous system may still suffer because of a trauma that happened years before your birth. Do you ever feel an overwhelming, deep-seated grief that has nothing to do with this lifetime? As if you are "crushed from the sorrowing", and breaking in pieces? Look to the lives of your parents and grand-parents. See where the story of your wounding began. You have taken this on to heal in your own life as there has been a resonance between you. Wounding that happened to ancestors seeks freeing in further generations. However, they need to own their own experiences and choices and until and unless they do, they remain un-whole, and not becoming whole, they remain undone. Although I do not live exactly the traumas and the heartaches of my ancestors, the trauma reaction and the wound reopening remain in me until I heal it.

Root Problems Affect the Whole Tree

Grandfather oak
Grandmother yew
Rooted deep in nature's womb
Sap like poured out sun
That flows through their veins
Streams golden to our hearts
All dammed up now
Closed tight shut
To life force fluid
These parched black eyes
No longer feel their way
To creation's wonders
But stay blind
To light of day and die
For too much searching.

What lurks in the roots of your family tree? Look at the present so-called problems in your life. Are they reflections from the past; your past in the form of your ancestors? What were the traumas? Money problems, sexual dysfunction, rages, marital problems, sicknesses, sudden deaths, disappointments, abortions, still-births, mother dying at childbirth, alcoholism or addictions, religious abuse that your family experienced?

Where there are deep rooted problems, look to the way you make choices. How do you decide what is good for you? Do you decide from a place of unconscious resonance with a dead relative; your aunt never married so you decide not to marry out of *misguided* affiliation to this relative? (*Family Constellations* by Bert Hellinger.) Maybe your mother did not marry the man she loved, as her parents would not allow it, so you, out of solidarity for your mother, did not marry the man you love. We often make choices from a place of bondage, not from a place of true freedom. And each choice we make from a place of unconsciousness has unproductive consequences. Or maybe you choose from a place of self-righteousness. Choices made from revenge, non-clarity or self-ishness end up very unproductive and at best, unhappy outcomes.

Choices we make from fear of course, do not serve us. Freedom to choose means I am conscious of the facts and accept the conse-quences. Therefore I am responsible. The problem is that we are not fully conscious of the facts, as they are hidden deep in the past of our family tree. The family that holds secrets, holds also the key to releasing those secrets to live more abundantly and free. My intention when choosing has to be free from revenge and a wish to cause suffering to another as well.

The Reptilian Brain

I believe that unconscious choice is influenced by the reptilian, automatic reactive survival brain. The development of the reptilian brain, also known as old grandfather, stem or root brain, takes place in the first trimester in the womb. All ancestral unfinished whole-making gets handed down to us and the reptilian brain is the receptacle of such unfinished business. The Christian Church teaches that because of the sin of Eve, our first mother, we are born into her original sin. Are we therefore born into the original traumas and dysfunctional lives of our parents and ancestors? I ask this question without judgement or blame because we are made in the likeness of Love itself and we have experiences to live out and past consequences to live too. In the end, all is stirred back into the Love from which we came. It's the stirring that we don't like so much, so if there is nothing to stir then all is very well.

What an amazing support the reptilian brain is to us human beings, helping to regulate the body systems and make sure that all internal functions work in harmony. What a truly marvellous conductor of the orchestra of our physicality. The instinctual self lives in the reptilian brain with its unbelievable safeguarding of our daily lives. The first three chakra energy centres are magnif-icent in their support of us, protecting us from all kinds of imaginary attacks. They guard us against any hurt that might come our way in the form of past remembrances. The instinctual self houses the earth/ego mind, it therefore acts not only in an automatic way, but also houses the unconscious.

All that represents the past has its space in the reptilian brain. Ancestral trauma resides here. Existential fear and addictions of all kinds live here. When the emotional-feeling creative brain can embrace, welcome and honour the reptilian, tribal brain energy, the reptilian self offers itself for healing. But it cannot heal us as it only knows conditional love. It cannot be creative as it has no idea about creative imagination. It has never learnt this.

It has been with us since the beginning of our evolution and much has been absorbed by the more recently evolved higher cortex in the meantime. It has taken millions and millions of years to establish itself and its job is really about survival, territory, tribal thinking and old belief systems that do not serve us any longer. When we can have compassion for this old friend and give gratitude to it for having looked after us for so long, it begins to soften and opens to another way of being in us.

Get in the habit of gently massaging it, touching it during the day with gentle hands and speaking to it about it being ok to feel your pain and your grief. Let it know that this is the way to heal. See a letter I wrote to my reptilian, or ego brain, in my book, *Let Love In*. When you can look at your ancient self through the eyes of Love, you can heal the past and feel free to let Love into the parts longing to be included. Otherwise you will continue to be a stranger to yourself and live in fear of the outer strangers. Let our dear hearts open to the Universal Heart and feel its Love and compassionate pulsating in our own small emotional holding.

When I become a stranger to my own heart, it blocks all possibility to receive love from another. Modern songs talk about giving our hearts to another but this is self-abandonment and self-neglect. My heart is meant to support me, and in turn be cared for, by me. This is not the responsibility of another. Neighbours said of my mother, "She gives her heart to everyone; she is a saint." This is not so holy when children need mothers to be present to themselves, so that they can be there for the children. And from a place of self-care it is easy to reach out and be there for another, but self-care comes first. Can I today welcome the tribal brain, my reactive self into the huge Universal Heart for safe-keeping? Otherwise I abandon myself, and my care for another is conditional.

The reptilian brain holds collective unhealed energy from tribal belief systems (see Bruce Lipton's book *The Biology of Belief*). Fight, flight or freeze is its default position, always. I do believe that strong emotions are held fast in the lower energy centres in the body and if they are never released into the heart for feeling and expressing, the lights in the nuclei of the cells dim and become sick as our thoughts affect our cellular system. Emotions need to move upwards towards the heart for release. There are six natural feelings which when not allowed to find expression, become dysfunctional:

Anger is natural and is a way to say no to what is not acceptable in one's life or in society. When it has never been expressed it becomes rage. Rage when not healthily outed can cause us to:

• Loathe ourselves
• Gossip about others
• Self-sabotage
• Become embittered
• Judge others
• Curse at life
• Blame everyone and everything for our unhappiness
• Become passive and actively aggressive
• Our body can suffer from liver problems, colon problems, headaches, high blood pressure, over-eating, bulimia and self-harming.

Fear is natural and is a way to be cautious about dangers. When it is not allowed to be expressed it becomes mental illness. We live consistently with:

- Phobias
- Anxieties
- Neurosis
- Traumatic reactions
- Isolation
- Apathy
- Mistrust in life itself
- Our body can suffer from lung infections, allergies and itchy skin.

Jealousy is a natural feeling. It simply says "me too, I would love that". When it is not expressed:

- It becomes envy so we hurt another to get our needs met.
- We learn to be overly competitive.
- We drive ourselves to succeed.
- We become self-seeking and self-absorbed.
- We reject others who are creative and seem to be getting on well in their lives.
- We set ourselves and others unreachable goals.
- We laugh in the face of another's downfall.
- Our body suffers eye problems, throat pain, blood pressure problems, stomach and liver problems, insomnia and irritable skin rashes.

Love is natural. It is meant to be shared with others and allows for bonding. Natural Love creates spaces for harmony and grace. It is not self-absorbed, and is inclusive rather than exclusive. Love that has never been expressed naturally becomes:

- Pity and self-absorption
- Conditional and obsessive
- Possessive
- Critical, smothering
- Abusive and sarcastic

- Disregarding of boundaries of others
- A means of using so-called "love" to seduce
- Sentimental and nostalgic
- Wild statements such as "only you can give me joy"
- The body can suffer from eating disorders, immobility, painful joints, heart problems and breathing problems.

Grief is natural. It is a way of expressing our losses with one another and it is meant to be shared. Grief that has never been expressed becomes:

- Sympathy and melancholy
- Stuck in self-absorption
- Isolated from other feelings
- Grievances and bitterness
- Leaking tears inappropriately
- Overwhelmed by the death of others
- Always looking inwardly with no outside contacts
- Needy and wanting
- Childish and fearful of being alone
- Always active
- Exhaustion
- Non-stop working
- Drinking too much to hide pain
- Depression and feeling oppressed
- Wanting to end it all now
- Body can suffer from headaches, bowel problems, stomach problems, insomnia and self-abuse.

Sexuality is natural and is a way to take pleasure in the body and to share this with another, if so desired. It is also for the continuation of procreation. Sexuality that has never been expressed becomes:

- Frigidity
- Inability to be creative

- Self-disgust
- Pornography
- Self-harming
- Sexual deviancy
- Seeing sexuality as sinful
- Represses sexual thought
- Disrespects another's sexual boundaries
- Body can suffer from colon problems, allergies, lung problems, teeth problems, headaches, migraines and breathing problems.

(Conscious celibacy is different and may be a healthy option when one chooses it.)

These natural feelings when expressed appropriately help us to live more congruent lives and make healthy choices and help create communities that care for one another and for the planet. If our ancestors felt deep helplessness then we consistently live victim consciousness, and if we do not explore our worlds of feelings, we simply repeat their tribal beliefs. We do this by carrying on the dysfunctions of the past. This is the inheritance we leave for our children's children to the fourth and seventh generation. Body illnesses can also be attributed to the state of mental health of our loved ones who passed to another life.

Don't forget, you are as free as your past is free. Our family may heal with us as may our ancestors but we do not insist. We simply heal our lives so that we change. But we have to take the first step. Maybe you are the one in your family constellations that has done or is still doing that right now. You cannot heal the family tree but your contribution to heal your own life contributes to change in the whole family dynamics. That is the power of one person becoming conscious. That is the way of love. We have to mind our own healing business and not get entangled in the family's need to heal. I have one life to heal and that is mine. The magic is that when I do heal, others have a chance to heal too. But the choice is theirs.

Here is a poem about the sap or gifts from our family tree. The gifts are there but we have to open to them. If we continue blaming we will never be able to receive the richness also present.

Healing Sap
We stand
With feet
Sure in the flow
Of their sap
Laden with
Life's potentials

Fluid rivers
Stream between us
Between us and them
With open heart I drink deep
From the flow
Again and again and again
With a song of gratitude singing my bones alive.

The sap from the tree was named liquid gold by alchemists such as Paracelsus and Hildegard of Bingen. Without this watery sugar, full of minerals and nutrients, the tree could not be nourished and would dry up, thus affecting its leaves and fruits. This sap is likened to the blood flowing in the veins of humans.

The sap flows from the roots of the tree to the whole tree. Aided by this suction force, water is drawn through the tree to replenish the sap. The tree may leak its sap because of a bacterial growth called wet wood or slime flux rendering it poor in nourishment. The sap leaks from cracks in the bark of the tree, drying it out and causing it to age prematurely. The disease needs to be treated from the roots so that the whole tree can be strengthened.

What was the potential sap that flowed through your own family tree from grandparents to parents to you? Can you name the talents and gifts available to you from your family tree?

What was the wet wood, the slime flux that prevented you from receiving the sap? Will you name the dysfunctions in your tree? If I am not aware of the wet wood in the tree I cannot heal it and I cannot access the golden elixir, the potential for creativity.

Exercise

- ~ Name the wet wood.
- ~ See your resonance with it in your life now, your reactions.
- ~ Honour and share the awareness.
- ~ Do a community ritual.
- ~ Show gratitude and bow to ancestors for gifts hidden in the wet wood.
- ~ Integrate the wet wood. Welcome it in deeper so that it gets healed.

Fruits from the Family Tree
If the roots be not pure
How may the sap flow?
If the sap does not flow
The fruits appear not
Then barren be the landscape
Of the soil of the family tree
Then barren be the landscape
Of the soul of the ancestors.

You have already looked at the wet wood and dysfunctions together with the rich sap and gifts handed down to you from your family tree. Where you feel a resonance with certain gifts it may be because there is the same or like gift in you that is awaiting awakening. You must not try to realize an ancestor's dream. It is very important that you realize your own. Gifts not realized rot in the soil of the family tree and can cause further generations to experience only dry rot where the possibility of rich talents could have enriched them. It takes courage and a sense of your own creative juices to venture into the field of self-expression. It takes support from the community to strengthen one's own will and heart to move into the flow of the sap of creativity.

What holds you back from living the amazing grace you are? Have you listened only to the earth mind or ego that tries, bless it, to keep you from venturing out there, deeper into the community, telling you that you will fail, you'll make a fool of yourself or you'll not make it?

You have to decide to which voice you listen. It is up to you.

Enlightenment
To sense the light of grace
We need to scrape the blind
From off our inner eyes
To know the light of grace
We need an awakened messiah
One that speaks not in our stead
But one that teaches us
To listen to our own known voice
And follow it to freedom.

Enlightenment Manifested Physiologically

The above poem suggests that we need to be shown how to go within and be led by our own inner wisdom. The wisdom hidden in our biological and spiritual DNA which will be made visible when we scrape the blindness from off our inner eyes, and instead of following an outer guide, are led by our own intuition.

Enlightenment is usually associated with the Buddhist idea of Nirvana; that state of bliss and peace reached by following the path of freedom mapped out by Gautama Buddha. A place or state of consciousness where the earth mind and all the suffering it calls forth is healed into pure Love. This cannot be accessible until and unless we have cleared our psychological baggage. Then we can live more integrated and joyful lives. We will no longer be driven by the earth/ego mind, but soulfully guided.

What we are saying is that enlightenment or awakening not only affects the inner states of mind but has a very direct affect on our physiology. By becoming more light-full in our minds, our bodies which are animated by life force will also be greatly affected. This is true healing which can affect not only oneself but can help the ancestors who wish to heal with us.

Up to now, we have all done much work on healing the dysfunctional programmes of the past and the shadows passed on to us via our ancestral lines. Although there will always be something to heal whilst we are still in bodies, we can still reach a place of inner peace and joy and operate from a place of integrity rather than that of suffering and attachment to old beliefs. Having integrated the exquisite instinctual animal self we will naturally move into a deeper sense of our divine self. We will evolve from instinctual awareness to intuitive living. That extraordinary animal self will have gathered insights and gut knowing that can be of tremendous help and assistance to the intuitive self. Gratitude to that self that has persevered with us for centuries upon centuries, often taking second place in the spiritual family of things.

I often say to people that we do not have to learn to be spiritual, for we are already that. We have to learn to integrate our base animal instinctual selves so that they do not prevent our evolutionary movement throughout our psyche. When we try to control or worse still, try and abolish our animal selves and deem them unspiritual or unworthy, we cannot be whole.

We learnt in biology class that the nucleus in the cells in the body is the centre of light in the cell; it is the heart or the main director or motivator for the cell. I believe that the nucleus consists of light particles which constitute all creation. So the same divine life force in which we live, move and experience life activates all creative phenomena. We have something very important in common with all created phenomena; at the centre of us all is the spark of Love itself.

When we consider the millions of cells in the physical form, then we can imagine the potentiality for light and for true liberty in the whole body. When the mind is healthy and free from reactive influences the body naturally emits great electric inspirational energy. The outer auric field of such a person transmits harmony and well-being to all creation. It is good to be around such a being. We say that they are full of energy and life. We are magnetically attracted to their aura field.

The opposite is said of a person who is not at peace within. Often I find many so-called spiritual people are against this or that. They say things like, "I'm against war", "I'm against cruelty to animals", etc. The energy of "being against" is very powerful. It flows throughout the nervous system and the heart is filled with war-like energy and becomes defensive. We say that there is heaviness in their being. In other words, the cells of the body are neither enjoying, nor emitting healthy life force. We often say that the person needs to "lighten up" so to speak. When we see that a person is depressed and takes a lot of medication we sense a dulling of the life force and it is easy to see the lack of lustre in the sunken eyes of such a dear one.

So what is it that helps us to stay more light-some? What helps to boost the spiritual immune system and lighten up our hearts? We have heard of the physical immune system, which is the body system that helps us to remain well and strong in our physicality. If there is a physical immune system then there is surely a spiritual immune system also. As there is a double strand to the double helix, I believe that one strand is responsible for our physical well-being and the other is the spiritual strand supporting our spiritual well-being. Whatever helps to keep the light shining in the cells of our bodies also helps to strengthen the spiritual immune system.

A potent medicine for strengthening the spiritual DNA or immune system lies in the suggestion, "Whatever delights the heart feeds the soul." Do you know what delights your heart? How often do you feed your soul daily, or weekly? When we sing, dance, love, invent, create, inspire, delight in something or someone, walk in nature we feel uplifted, lightened up, we feel at one with ourselves and all beings. Our dear ego minds become quiet. We are not judging or reacting; we are being present to the now. We feel that we are worthwhile and that being here and now is such a gift. My own practice is heartfelt gratitude for each breath and being grateful that life chooses to flow throughout my system with ease and blessing.

All these feelings from the heart feed the soul and when the soul is fed thus, the spiritual immune system is supported and helped. The spiritual sap flows unimpeded from our ancestral line to our spiritual DNA and the centre of the nuclei in the cells is brought to homeostasis. The cerebral spinal fluid flows like a pure stream of light throughout the biology and a sense of well-being pervades the whole being. There is harmony and balance in the cellular structure again. We actually feel this state of healthiness in the body/mind and we are brought back into our innate natural state of inner peace and joy.

In the gospel of Matthew, Chapter 6:22-23, we read:

The (inner) eye is the lamp of the body.
If your eye is sound, your whole body will be full of light.
But if the (inner) eye is not sound, your whole body will be full of darkness.

This is saying that if your inner eye, your third eye is not full of light, the sap of spiritual energy is unable to flow through your energetic body and the life force becomes sluggish. Then you will live from your shadow and physiologically you will be ill. When this happens, we will add to the collective shadow, both within and without. So to bring healing and vibrant life to your whole body/mind and help in the healing of our planet, we must first be filled with light from within the cells of our own bodies. Integrating the dark shadows of our past helps to bring about health and healing in our beings.

The electromagnetic energy in our nervous systems and our hearts transmits healing charges. Endorphins are emitted to the blood circulatory system and we are fed light. When the heart and brain work together in harmony we have amazing power to create new inner and outer realities. We have the ability to change the neural transmitters in our brain thus promoting well-being in body/mind. So, to be well in our physicality it is important to be "lit up" from within. We need to practise doing this by creative visualization daily.

∽

Visualization: Let Love Heal … Now

Sit in a comfortable chair. Make sure you will not be disturbed for the next half hour or so.

Let the body be quiet and allow it to relax.

Let the breath come naturally, watching it deepening as you breathe easily. Notice how natural it is for the breath to slow down. Just notice if this is so for you.

Ahhhh. The breath will naturally let go with a light sound when it is fully relaxed. Just notice if this is so for you.

As you focus on your breath, see if you would care to direct it to your belly; right deep down into the belly.

The more you focus the breath here, the deeper it will go.

That's it … deep down so you can breathe in slowly and deeply.

And breathe out in the same way. Slowly and deeply breathe out with a light sound.

Notice how the breath follows your guidance.

Slowly in, deeply and slowly out with a light sound.

Good.

Breathe like this for the next five breaths.

Then pause and breathe naturally.

Take your own time now.

When you breathe like this, you are more and more open to oxygen, health, life force and inspiration.

Be open to breath in your life.

Be open to life in your breath.

Keep opening more and more.

Deeper and deeper into your belly.

And so the breath comes in from above your head. And you slowly focus it down through your body into your belly.

If you get distracted by other sounds around you, that's fine. Just slowly and without judgment return to the breath.

Slowly breathe in and slowly, with a slight sound, breathe out. All is well.

At this time, if there is a part of your body that needs focused loving attention focus the breath there. Focus the breath now to the part that is in need of loving attention.

Slowly awaken it to the loving compassion of the breath.

Your full breath is pure life force, and life force is Love.

It is your best friend; always there, always ready to support you, no matter what.

When you have identified the part of your body that needs this healing attention,

Imagine it opening to the breath.

Imagine it allowing the healing in. It is an invitation from the universe. To heal you from the inside out; the natural way of healing energy.

Keep focusing this loving energy. Focus it onto the part that longs for your kindness and loving attention.

Just like a hurt child will turn to its parent for love, your body also turns to you for healing.

Allow your body to be cared for. Allow it to be at rest;

let Love in, let Love flow, let Love heal.

Breathe deep, deep into the part that needs this focused Love.

Right now, the healing power of Love is seeping into the cells in your body, filling them with energy and life.

Each blood vessel,

Each nerve,

Each tiny cell

Is longing for this infusion of Love.

Let Love in now. Right now.

The healing power of Love is seeping into each muscle and sinew. All of the cells in your body are receiving this divine energy.

The divine flow.

This infusion is full of universal grace and well-being.

For the natural way of Love is healing, restorative and compassionate.

Breathe in this golden elixir for your whole being and for your whole body/mind.

Feel a surge of energy like a river flowing through your whole body. Feel well in all of you now.

Imagine this beautiful bright golden elixir flowing from the top of your head right down through the whole of your body down, down, down into your feet.

You are saturated in this river of mercy and kindness.

Your breath breathes in this golden stream directing and focusing it down into the whole of your being.

It refreshes, cleanses, reinvigorates, releases and re-creates the cells in your body/mind.

As you continue to breathe in this golden healing liquid your whole being awakens to the memory of Love and of being fully and wholly accepted for what you are. You are a divine being learning to be human. The *what* of you is divine and this divine self is what heals the *who* of you. When the personality is healed, you are made whole again; no separation and no more isolation. You are home.

Breathe deeply again and when you are ready, allow yourself to breathe naturally and gently without moving any other part of your body. Open your eyes and keep breathing gently and slowly as you take in the room. Only when you are ready, gently and slowly move your body into sitting and be here fully.

ͻ

Questions to Explore

- What were the traumas in your family tree, eg., sudden deaths, suicide, marrying outside religious beliefs, pregnancy before marriage (if this was known as sin), alcoholism, sexual abuse or incest that were kept secret?
- How did your family cope/deal with grief, anger, jealousy and sexuality?
- What were the gifts (sap) you received from your family tree?
- Did your parents or ancestors express their talents? Or were they hidden and not admired or encouraged?
- Did your ancestors carry guilt and shame?
- Do you feel a resonance with any of your dead relatives? Are any of their lives similar to yours?
- Whom do you mostly resemble in your family?
- Are you named after a dead relative?
- What diseases did your ancestors die of? Was there a tendency to heart failure or cancer?
- Was there a so-called black sheep in your family? Why?
- Was there someone they referred to as a saint, meaning they were good, forgot themselves to be present for others?
- Name the many graces you are grateful for in your day.

Chapter IV

The last Ecstasy

Dear one
Look inside and out
What you see is the landscape
Of your own thought
Have you danced upon the stones
That rawed your feet
Or bowed to the one
That shattered all your dreams
For you have angered when another
Stole your image of yourself
And planted a foreign being in its stead
The stone is not the fiend
Nor is the robber to be blamed
And the ones who burst your heart
Came at your own calling
Can you dear friend
Bow to the teacher in all things?

There is so much information known only by the ancient tribes and the indigenous peoples like the Celts, regarding the sacred rituals and initiations of living and dying. One such ritual that is not to be found in either the Christian or Buddhist teachings is "last ecstasy" or "the enlightenment through the physical at death". It is of these ancient, sacred rites of death passages that I write.

If the adages, "as above so below", "as within so without" and "as in the beginning so in the end" are true, then we have to look at how life force enlivens physicality in the beginning, in order to understand physicality without it at the end. I will leave this in-depth knowing about the creation story to learned biologists and like scientists, but I do know however that when we understand a little more about the earthing processes of in-bodied phenomena, we will hopefully get a better knowledge of the dying processes of the same.

My present interest is in getting to know more about the so-called end-of-life processes—although life does not end as such but transforms—as well as how we can become more and more consciously present to all it entails. That includes knowing all the time that we are in the midst of the sacred mysteries of birthing processes. I also know that the more spiritual knowledge we acquire about the birthing experiences, the better able we will be to truly assist and be present to our own deaths and the deaths of those around us.

I have spent some years working with and understanding a little more about death and dying. Indeed from the womb itself I have been taught about the mysterious and often incomprehensible spiritual processes of death and dying. I have spent my life learning from dying people and their families and when I began to work with Elisabeth Kübler-Ross in the 1990s, I began to see the purpose of my own life's work. Whilst I know that I will never fully comprehend the deeper mysteries of the processes of birthing and dying, it is good to at least ask deep questions, because I have found that the answers work themselves out in the living fully of my own life.

As a nun I tried to find some answers regarding the internal dying process and after-death beliefs according to Catholic theology. I am sad to report that I was not at all satisfied with the vague references to the afterlife with regards to heaven, hell and purgatory and a place called "limbo" for babies who were not baptized.

The more spiritual depths of sacred biological interchanges at the final stages of human life were not available to me and certainly, the theology of enlightenment was not referred to. Physicality was seen as a disadvantage to enlightenment. One had to deny one's incarnation in order to reach sainthood. This was Catholic dogma at that time and has not truly evolved since the second Vatican council in the late 1960s.

My experience and research has been that religions seem to treat the physical, our biology, as inferior to spirit. One must always "transcend the body as quickly as possible and get in touch with spirit". This is known as spiritual bypassing and no doubt this prevents full engagement with earth life itself and leaves us human beings forever in states of guilt, shame and fear.

The theology of spirit or mind being superior to mere form has left us bereft of ever reaching nirvana and has put spirit in such a hierarchical place that God Itself does not have a chance of getting to know humanity, its own wondrous creation, as there is no question of intimacy being afforded either.

This poem by a friend, Bethan Elsdale, talks about actually inhabiting the physicality and not abandoning it:

> As I inhabit my belly
> My legs reveal themselves
> Rooting downwards
> Connecting me to ground

Rising in receptivity
My diaphragm invites
A resting place for a grateful heart
Which might otherwise beat
To the timing of unmet grief
Ah! Here I am
Here I am
Yes God, here I am.

Religious dogmas give us little information about the sacredness of our physicality other than to preach that the body needs to be subservient to the spirit. As a nun I performed the practice of self-whipping in order to admonish the body for its sinfulness. We were told not to draw blood but I do know that a few of the more ardent nuns whipped themselves so that they did draw blood. This hatred of the self, became a practice in itself which for me, deteriorated into anorexia and self-abandonment. I know of a dear person who had suffered all her life from religious scruples who died in fear of not having truly abandoned bodily pleasures for the more spiritual pursuits of the soul.

How can such beliefs serve us as human beings? The answer clearly is that they don't. And what of our sacred sexuality? Adjectives such as sacred, divine, holy and worthy are not included in the Christian catechism when referring to human sexuality and orgasm. The subject itself is not expounded upon other than to relegate it to the realms of sinfulness and profanity, unless in reference to propagation of the so-called faithful when the sexual act was a necessary evil to be endured by women and a necessary release for the men. It is a subject not advanced by the holy fathers as their innate fear of Eros and all things to do with sensual physicality overrides any softening in their insistence of the ugliness of our sinful natures, encased and shamefully wrapped in flesh.

Imagine the horror in the minds of the hierarchy of the Church if they had to accept that a happy and holy death might include an orgasmic fusion of the physical and the spiritual? That which was at one in the beginning must surely return to the one in the end? The theory of entanglement according to the Christian Church seemed only to refer to matrimony. "What God has put together man must not pull asunder" was curiously used as a defence against divorce in the Catholic faith. To imagine our sexual nature fusing and consciously uniting with soul would not be accepted as a pious sacrament.

I have been allowed to experience whilst in meditation, that a so-called happy death can be initiated by sacred soul orgasm experienced physically and spiritually by the whole body/mind. I realized that a happy death was that sacred fusion of ego and soul, the return of the prodigal, so to speak, into the arms of soul. This is the Hieros Gamos or sacred marriage. I could see also that the birthing process could be an amazing experience of kundalini energy, flowing between mother and child in an explosive ignition of life force, resulting in the earthing of what was up until that moment, an un-incarnate being. Is it so difficult to imagine that birth and death could initiate such an all-encompassing blissful explosive experience for human beings?

I believe that these two uniquely intense and magnificent occurrences, unlike any other we will experience throughout life, should be marked by a fierce concentrative explosion of total ecstasy, the slow gathering momentum of the fire force, ignited by the strength of the fusion.

Tantra and Sacred Sexuality

When tantric practices are taught to people, in the way of guiding them to experience in-depth the sacrament of sacred sexuality, they are helped to get in contact with and experience an immense and powerful life force within themselves that was hitherto out of reach. The result of this mighty energy flow is initiated by deep visualization. Secretion of chemicals such as serotonin, dopamine and oxytocin or "sacred chemistry" from the fluids in the pineal gland is expressed physically by sensual releasing movements in the body. They begin in the feet and move upwards, to include not only the sexual organs, but the entire body/mind.

Tantra understands that the whole of a woman's body contains erogenous zones, whilst those of a man are centred more at the genital areas. Women's bodies are the temples of the Goddess, watched over by her. Therefore each part of a woman's body is likened to "a chalice of etherial graces, known only to the initiates and holy ones".

During tantric experiences each cell in the body/mind is engaged in the most intense pleasure and deeply focused contemplation known to humans. Because one is instructed and helped to get to know one's own body before they explore that of another, they can truly know various altered states of consciousness and utter peak experiences. In many cases holy oils are used on the body to open the pleasure fields to bless them and to add to the intensity experienced.

The ego mind bows to such powerful life force energy and the soul guides the practitioners in the path of total surrender. Centuries of learned stifled self-expression and shame, which have kept us separate from pleasure, is transformed so that only pure life force itself is present. This dear judgmental ego-self is welcomed into the still presence of soul and the two become one. I welcome myself home in me; the other welcomes themselves home in them so that there is only one of us. What then is present between us is pure Love. This sense of Love happens because of the body, not in spite of it. And the wonder is that the human beings engaged in this practice still remain attached to the earth elements and the soul cord so that they can return to the physical again. Of course as in all practices there can be abuse present also. One must therefore be aware of this and find a well-known ethical practitioner in whom one can place trust and respect before being guided into Tantra.

Dying: As Natural as Birthing

As in the beginning
So in the end
As in form
So out of form
As in life on earth
So in life in death
All is Life transitioning
All is Life transforming.

Returning again to the Near Death Experience I had in Northern Ireland in 1973, I experienced a deep sense of joy, peace and deep, silent relaxation whilst in the hospital bed. Whilst still aware of my body and witnessing it I felt, at first, a tingling flush through my system like a mighty wind. However the state of joy that carried me infiltrated my entire mind, and peace and harmony spread like a blazing fire in a forest. My body helped me in the process of deeply experiencing this, whilst I was out of it! I feel somehow that since this experience I have been able to view my own and others' physicality in a totally different way. I sensed that there was so much more to being in the flesh than just existing. The aliveness I experienced was something that I did not experience whilst fully in the body. It was as if I had to leave the restraints of the physical in order to view the whole scene from another angle! How unimportant it seemed to me that I should live or die. I was not at all involved with the outer scripts, or agendas. The inner journey, the inner scenery and landscape, was more important to me.

Of course during the actual dying process we are still involved in body consciousness; albeit not so deeply because the earth, fire, water, air and space elements take time to slowly leave physicality. This means that the body is slipping more and more into the energetic former template that contributed to forming the physicality. But the body is still the carrier of the elements until the last one has left. This is the process when one is dying from old age or natural causes and is the natural withdrawal procedure.

Dying is a natural act, as is birthing, meaning they are both from nature and nature is their guide. But we have introduced too much medical intervention so that these natural processes have become dishonoured. Mother knows instinctively when the baby is ready for earthing as the child's hypothalamus emits the signal and she answers. Her body knows how to be. The dying also know this natural act of decathexing when the pineal gland secretes the death hormone. But now we introduce so many unnatural procedures and so much medical intervention, that that which is natural becomes disjointed and eventually the natural gets lost in dogmatic, intrusive medicine.

It is wonderful to hear a newborn baby open her lungs and take her first breath and make her first real strong earth sound. She is experimenting with engaging in her humanity as an earthed being. Having experienced the orgasm of birthing she needs peace, quiet, gentle holding, soothing sounds in order to truly begin the cathexing journey into incarnation. In the first years she will cathex even more in order to feel her place in the family of created phenomena.

Likewise the dying will feel this difficulty of adjusting to being dead if the process of dying has been disruptive and intrusive. We only need to intervene when physical pain becomes too intrusive so that the dying cannot focus on the journey of decathexing. And this stage of decathexing takes its own timing as it penetrates the layers of human grounding and conditioning to eventually reach the place of innocence.

In the case of the earthing baby and the dying, decathexing other, the body is vulnerable and naturally needs unobtrusive attention from caring persons to make sure they are comfortable and have their meta needs met with loving tender care and not much physical intervention. The baby coming into earth life and the dear form leaving it, are undergoing tremendous catharsis, the most unimaginable alchemy and the most intense adventure they will ever know. Neither will remember these passages of intense consciousness until next time they engage in either of these adventures at a deeper level with themselves. The old ones maintain that at birth we have an internal knowing regarding the journey ahead but it gets misted over by earth experiences. They also maintain that we know the way out of the earth since we have already experienced this so many times. The trauma of both birth and death robs us of the facility of remembering. There is a poem (translated from the Irish) about this:

> so many times I've come
> so many times I've left
> yet time after time
> in the mist of time
> that faint trickle of memory
> lies numb in timelessness

When does this memory of coming and going get lost in us? Does the tiny newborn know the future it has chosen in the recess of the cellular system and is this knowledge accessible? In the so-called mist of time does the tiny being get a glimpse of the future and if so, does it maybe sometimes decide to withdraw its willingness to be earthed and return to source? Maybe she has incarnated too quickly, too impulsively and needs to wait for another womb to bear her at another time.

It is such a journey to take, from source to form each time. The elements have to settle into the child's system. The organs and heart flow also need to establish themselves in this new container for life force. It takes time for the form to fully arrive in physicality. From template to density takes time. The heart in us has to grow into the sacred heart, this is about experiencing our humanity in the safekeeping of the Universal Heart. I often wonder what it must be like for the child coming in, what the ground of the mother feels like in comparison to her own; what the outside of the mother's form feels like, senses like, compared to the inside of her. Such a sense of grief for the newborn… Such a sense of loneliness and isolation. Once so close, so involved with mother; now on the outside, in a very large, extended space with other breaths to deal with, other touches to encounter, other voices to absorb, other handling to get used to. What a brand new noisy, very bright world this must be for the little one having just left the knowing, dark cave of safety and the deeply known rhythms of mother's inner world.

There needs to be more honouring, more attention given to and more consciousness applied to the birthing of small beings into this very large, aggressive world. Likewise there needs to be more sensitive considerations of the beings leaving this world.

Spiritual teacher, Alice Bailey, in her book *Death the Great Adventure* says, "The prison house of the flesh is dissolved by the *slow* withdrawing of the light and life", suggesting that the dissolution needs time just as cathexing needs time. And these experiences are forerunners for the next phase or stage of life whether coming into or leaving form. Here, however, I am concentrating on the dissolution of the elements and the decathexing of the form.

Before death sets in, the dying person will experience very intense sensations as the elements start to dissolve. The emotional quadrant does not serve us at this stage as it is absorbed into full consciousness away from earth mind. In the *Tibetan Book of Living and Dying*, the author Sogyal Rinpoche explains, "On the whole, existence is determined by the elements; earth, fire, water, air and space. Through them our body is formed and sustained and when they dissolve, we die. This is very clear." So the physical, emotional and mental dissipate until in the end, there is only the spiritual left. In my NDE I was interested to discover that I was not as emotionally involved with my two-year-old daughter as I certainly would have been were I fully present in my emotional being. This I questioned for some time until I fully realized that as the life force is withdrawing, our internal states of consciousness adapt to the changes. I marvelled at how the whole body assists the life force to leave, a kind of internal compassionate cooperative.

This is the very reverse of the cathexis stage of personality development where the physical, instinctual, emotional and mental stages develop and the intuitive and spiritual growth follows. Of course we are from Source and we have to also evolve spiritually throughout the incarnation. We cannot *become* more spiritual, rather we choose to let our spiritual-self infiltrate the rest of our personality, until we become infused with inspiration.

> Know dear one
> The song of death
> Dreams the birth of creation
> As beloved life
> Embraces your heart
> She is planning on leaving
> In the heart
> Of the seed there
> Hides the fullness of mystery
> In the same seed
> Hides the destroyer
> Of all that is created
> So live within
> The heart of death
> And die fully into birth.

Extreme Unction: The Last Rites

In the Christian belief system the baptism of a young child into the Church, culture and family of belonging is the first sacrament she receives. Witnesses are gathered to name the child and welcome them in. The anointing of the dying or last rites of passage is the one received at the end of life helping the dying to detach and helping the witnesses to say goodbye. It is usually at this stage of dying that the Catholic priest or minister is called to administer the last rights to the dying person to help the soul leave the form happily. Often if the person is coherent, the priest will ask them to confess their sins. If the person is unable to connect verbally, as I was during a Near Death Experience, the priest will offer absolution for all their sins. I was, however, in a place of joy and would have been happy to have died then. However my time had not yet come.

The holy oils used in the past were those of jasmine, pure olive oil and myrrh. The crown of the head, the eyes, forehead and between the eyes; the nose, ears, mouth, throat, heart, hands and feet were all blessed. Shamans however believe that these oils were used to facilitate the energy flow of the auric bodies enabling these centres to open to grace. This blessing with holy oils was to prepare the dying for the final bliss or final ecstasy. When we look to the oils used for anointing in the past, we are told that jasmine helps to arouse the sexual, kundalini serpent energies. Together with other oils these are known as "the oils of the holy spirit". It would be interesting to know if priests nowadays know about the ancient esoteric meaning behind the use of the holy oils. Shamans certainly do. They talk about the seven fields of ripening or the seven openings into spirit. Jesus spoke of the seven mansions of grace. If by means of these oils the energy centres are encouraged to expand, then it has to be to facilitate the energetic flow of life force.

As the physical becomes almost dissolved, the auric body that holds emotionality and experience expands into the environment. Consciousness expands at death as soul is reaching her climactic triumph. Whilst outwardly one sees a shrunken body form, internally a most unbelievable mystery is taking place on a spiritual level.

The Saints and Ecstasy

The Catholic Church exhibits various extremely sensual pictures of saints such as St. Teresa of Avila, St. Margaret, Mary, and St. Terese of Liseaux in what was known as "experiencing the sacred ecstasy". These women of the Church were so at one, so fused with their beloved Jesus, that they suffered unbearable bliss. The pictures I have seen in various churches and convents, no doubt give credence to these words. These women were clearly experiencing out-of-body experiences depicted by the facial and body expressions that were named "petit mort", meaning "little death". Indeed it seems they were fully united with their internal lover. This could be what is called the *Hieros Gamos*: the internal holy marriage or the union within themselves of yin/yang, anima/animus.

These women and some male saints such as John of the Cross and Ignatius, may have been experiencing kundalini orgasms, a deep pulsation of life force throughout their forms aided by the flow of pure joy from the bliss hormones. The suggestion that these sainted women and men might have been engaged in kundalini practice would not have been accepted by the Church, yet it is no less sacred than being in deep contemplation. The apostles were said to appear drunk after they had the initiation of the deep fire force of spirit baptism.

When the Christian Church separated Eros from sacred practice, aridity and sterility set in. I lived this acrid space for too long. Carolyn Myss who is an author and medical intuitive, named this state "monastic without a monastery".

The Final Ecstasy: The Soul Prepares to Leave

will you just let me be
when the soft light dawns
will you walk with quiet feet
when the soft light dawns
will you speak my name as silk worm creeps
with bowing form
when the soft light dawns
and will you not look away
if your eyes behold the wonder

as my silent hallelujah
shouts its glad and splendid chorus
when the soft light dawns
for you cannot reach me now
nor can I turn to you
the door is opening now
and I walk through

When the person who has led a conscious, soulful life reaches this stage of dying, they will experience what could be called pure ecstasy, a spiritual orgasm that affects not just the genitals but the entire body form. At the stage when the fire is dissolving one might imagine that the dying person is in pain as the face contorts, the mouth opens, the arms may flail and involuntary reflexes may jerk the body. Often before this stage the dying person may actually seem to get better. They look younger, may even say some words and maybe even say they have met loved ones that have died before them. This is a real sign that death is imminent. When pain relief is given at this stage one will experience shock and terror as the body/mind and soul are so alive and whole at this stage. Soon the final moments will come and the inner adventure is about to start.

The death hormone is now infiltrating the whole being; the soul is being totally freed and is elated. Form is no longer a burden, freedom is nigh. The great hallelujah will soon be sounded and they will hear it internally. They will be called back to Source. To explain this final stage of death I ask you to imagine one is having a sexual orgasm and is interrupted by someone coming into the room and shaking their body or asking questions. The shock is quite painful as one is in a state of higher awareness and altered state of consciousness, super-charged with electro-magnetic soul energy and then they have to quickly adjust to ordinary consciousness again. The same may also be said about the birthing process when the child is about to come in to the earth and the joy and bonding is experienced by mother and child. Too much pain relief can interfere with this sacred process and too much touching and movement away from mother can be devastating for the child.

Physical outward manifestations complementing those experienced in sexual orgasm will affect the dying form. The face may contort, mouth may open, various reflexes in the muscles may jerk and the physical body may seem to be writhing in pain. I have often heard sounds emitted from the voice box at this stage too. These are not voluntarily voiced but are the result of involuntary throat muscle reflexes. These sounds may have been voiced as natural sexual expressions if the bliss cocktail was allowed to flow unimpeded throughout the whole being. This experience of spiritual and sacred orgasm engulfs the whole of the astral body/mind and one sinks into a state of amazing grace.

If at this stage a doctor prescribes more pain relief this will dull consciousness more and more, leaving many dear ones unconscious during the most important part of the dying process. And as I have said of the birthing process, too much interference also prevents one from actually dying as they are brought back into the physicality again and again, often seen in resuscitation of old people. It is very important that we learn more about the dying processes so that we may live lives with more awareness and love. The more evolved we are spiritually at the time of death, the more joy we can experience in the dying process. We even have the chance to finally leave the form in a state of absolute bliss, leaving the whole energetic being aflame with divine love.

When people who are not so far evolved on the journey of love die, they do not experience this orgasmic death. Rather they die before the energy has reached the heart energy. That is fine for that state of consciousness. If they had never experienced real bliss during life, to experience it fully at death might be too frightening. We get the death we are prepared to die. Some might even die in fear if they experience too much bliss. For more advanced souls—there is no judgement in that statement—the ideal is for the soul to leave form through the top of the head, not the solar plexus or even from the physical heart centre. The emotional love has to be transformed in the fires of the Universal Heart which transforms it into harmony and balance.

How we leave the form this time will affect how we enter into our next experience of life out of form. This in turn affects the energy with which we return to the earth plane. May we return to earth having evolved spiritually so that our love will be more altruistic and our compassion more outwards-reaching.

Aíte after Death

If love be not your desire
Then die now
And come not again
Till you have tasted wisdom
For until you burn with love
You will be troubled
And be a trouble.
So, when your soul takes clay again
Let your heart burn into it
And rent the seas apart
With the force of your passion
So that life may raise you
In total magnificence.

Being able to adapt to a change of environment without losing our centre is of great importance in the dying process. Many are stuck in the place of ease, a so-called security: comfortable, non-challenging, non-risky, non-changing, predictable and habitual. This is based mostly on fear. They do not find it easy to make the leap of faith to visualize a life without form and are afraid of not having their material needs met. To be able to shift from form to non-form, from body to spirit will be the challenge after death. If we get too attached to material things they drag us down. Those who live soulfully, die fully into soul.

Getting used to following your soul's journey is the way of paradox and symbolism whilst in form. It will be automatic, plain sailing for you when you have left it. Why not welcome change? The capacity for being grateful for all the gifts of experience, without guilt, is the gift of old age. One can then more easily look forward to the great adventure which confronts us in death. In your highest moments, when you engage with soul, you realize that change, transition and transformation are necessary for the continuation of life. Life is not dependent on form for its vitality and movement. Your own soul will lead you into the greatest adventure of all, the adventure into death and the experiences you will encounter after death. As below, so above.

The "Aíte" or "bardos" refer to life on earth and life after this life. It is advisable to live consciously so that we can die in the same energy. For a more comprehensive reading on the Aíte see my book, *A Celtic Book of Dying*, however I give a condensed version here.

Aíte and Dream Walking

Dream said the old woman
Dream wide like the sea
And have a mind to keep free
From all unlit fires of small desires
Ashed from a past of all
That did not last
Let your dream fly
Singing you to all the songs
That long for sound relief
Dream heaven here and now
And send it straight to Tir Na N-og
So it can welcome you
When you breathe it out.

In Celtic tradition the dream time was a very important agent of information as it mirrored the awake time. It mirrored our inner state of consciousness back to us. The idea was that all experience is an expression of our dream; all experience is a projection of our inner story. They believed that as within, so without regarding the dream. In other words, our thoughts become flesh and dwell in us as reality.

The birthing process was seen as a series of passages or "Aíte" or "bardos" through which we had to pass in order to get to the fulfilment of the dream. We had to experience the long tunnel of the birth canal not knowing where it would lead us. The confusion of separateness, alienation and *spaciousness* caused us, as not yet born babes, to experience a sense of abandonment. As if the womb had abandoned us and we were alone with too much space once birthed.

What our senses experienced then still resound in the echoes of primal memory. Did we get a preview of the life before us? Was it scary for us as tiny beings not yet accustomed to form and solidity? Would we have to experience pain and suffering to reach the light outside this cave of darkness?

When the final stage came, we gave the signal to mother that we were coming, "Get ready, and open the door to earth life." Mother then released us. Did we feel in that moment of release also some rejection? Mother no longer felt the pain and suffering but instead pure joy and pure ecstasy. At the end of a long journey, did we feel it too, as we looked into her loving eyes and were held softly, close to her skin as we breathed in earthiness? In that moment it would seem that the journey was forgotten. Or was it?

Aíte of Release

When one dies consciously, it is a glorious experience as we are prepared to leave the earth having no desire to look back. There is no unfinished business to hold us back and we adjust to being out-of-body life. For many this is not an easy passage as perhaps they suffered in dying or in not being prepared to let go and were holding on to materialism. Perhaps fear overtook them when the breath laboured. Some will actually wonder if they had died and look around for the body.

The astral body may still hang on to earth life, perhaps around the home or to a loved one, not wanting to be released. Relatives can also hold their dead from fully leaving if they keep screaming for them. This is difficult for the dear soul passing as they may be drawn back to earth, albeit in an astral way without substance.

Aíte of Peace and Tranquillity

Here we can relax after the long journey out of earth life. People who had had a lot of pain before dying can avail of deep rest and peace before they pass on to the next Aíte. Those who caused only pain to others will experience this pain state now and there will be no peace. The hell experienced is not inflicted by another. It is self-hatred that imposes these states of consciousness. When we can begin to release the blame and feel the sorrow, we can move on, but not until then. The laws of the universe are such that balance and harmony must prevail. It is not personal.

Aíte of Review

This is a stage of looking back on the life lived and this is done literally in the wink of an eye as in this dimension there is no time or space. All happens in the now of eternity. Each thought, word, deed, intention and dream is again made available to us and the times when we loved unconditionally and sent compassion to all beings bring us again deep joy. Likewise, the pain we caused another will be made manifest in us and in this dimension there is nothing we can do to redo this. We will undergo the suffering we caused in another.

It helps if this can all be done through the eyes of compassion and balance with no judgement. As we may go into regret and wish we could undo the pain we caused, if we are able to ask forgiveness now, there is a chance for healing. When we hurt another here and now, it is so important to speak our sorrow and say how we wish we had not done this. To hold on to regrets and remorse is not helpful here or in the hereafter. Let us do something about our regrets before we die. And let us do so with compassion for all beings, not forgetting to include ourselves.

Aíte of Projection

All experience is a projection of our inner story. There will be many chances for us to learn from the wise souls who departed before us. Elisabeth Kübler-Ross told me she hoped to see Albert Einstein and Carl Jung and Victor Franklin after she died. She so loved the research done by these men and she felt a great resonance with them. I would also love to be with the consciousness of Carl Jung when I die. There will be numerous chances to continue our learning before we earth ourselves again.

As non-incarnated beings, we will have chances to learn and gain wisdom every day after death from this lifetime, just as we would as incarnated beings. It will depend on our state of awareness. When we are ready to incarnate again we will do so with help from the world of our healed and unhealed past life. If each earth life is a progression and spiritual evolution, our soul will choose the best parents and family constellation wherein to be born again.

In this place we have an overview of all the experiences we have had and many regret their actions of non-love. At this stage, self-mercy and compassion are needed so that we can move through the other Aíte. This is the same in life. We cannot move deeper into our dream if we are holding self-non-love. Self-acceptance and love help us to experience the various Aíte or passageways of life and death.

Aíte of «Glindar» or Deep Joy

When the earth mind has been welcomed and loved into the Universal Heart, soul receives it with joy and the two become one. The holy internal marriage has happened. This is the great hallelujah, the continuity of the last ecstasy I shared earlier. From the state of divine grace, saints have taken on the work of inspiring us on earth. As they are fully in spirit they delight in doing so.

When the earth mind is still controlling, the Aíte is Other. There is no God standing in judgment. We, by our own wills and choices, create our worlds whether in the world of earth or spirit. We are the co-creators with the universe; we are the dreamers who awaken to our own dream making. This is the time for awakening from the dream, for wakening one another into what we had dreamed together.

Celtic consciousness shows us that what is dreamed within needs to be earthed without. In other words, our thoughts become flesh and dwell in us as reality. So be careful what you dream.

> The passageway is dark
> And no one calls my name
> Save my own dream
> That gently opens me
> To my own heart's longing
> And I, used to seeing into the dark
> Open wide my eyes
> And run naked towards the dream
> And see it run towards me.

Consciousness and Organ Donation

In the last 50 years much research has been done in the field of death and dying by people like Alice Bailey, Dr Elisabeth Kübler-Ross, Raymond A. Moody, Stephen Levine and Denis Purcell. Alice Bailey, in her book *Death: The Great Adventure* writes, "…that something survives the process of death and that something persists after the disintegration of the physical body, is steadily being proved." This *something* of which she writes must then transcend physicality. Perhaps that is the mysterious quality referred to in the Christian bible: "In it we live and move and have our being."

Gregg Braden, in his book *The God Code*, names this *it* as "consciousness". According to Alice Bailey, it is consciousness that both maintains all life and into which all life dissolves at death. So it seems that consciousness is the prevailing energy that sustains both life on earth and life without form. It includes the life energy of all created phenomena. I have written before that life is not dependent on form so the obvious question then is, what is consciousness?

In the 1950s when I was at school, scientists believed in the phenomenon of empty space. This is not now the case. Those named above have explored in depth, the idea of an intelligence beyond that of the brain that Gregg called the "God Code" which until now was the study and preoccupation of theologians and "holy men". That seemingly was their sphere of investigation whilst that of the scientist was to concentrate on verifiable matter. Now there is more cooperation between the disciplines to produce a more coherent outcome with a possibility of science and religion asking similar questions while using different languages to articulate their findings. This is exciting and useful for us all.

So what then is consciousness? Old yogis such as Sat Chit Ananda would say that *all* is consciousness, there is nothing but consciousness. Scientists might say that nothing is really solid and there is an energetic backdrop to all created phenomena. This is in effect saying that behind all density is energy. Gregg Braden says that the space between us is consciousness, energy. There is no such thing as nothing or empty space. When we delve into the world of energy we are then entering into the realm of metaphysics. And here we have to stay whilst investigating our own physicality.

If one describes consciousness as pure electromagnetic, untainted, unconditioned yin/yang, anima/animus, male/female energy, the fusion of out-breath/in-breath, the spiralling perfect movements of resonance/disharmony, attraction/revulsion, one can imagine how the language from one state of consciousness does not fit another! One has to be at ease with paradox in order to transcend ordinary logic and linear thinking. For we have to go beyond our conceptual awareness to be able to create a space for understanding. And in doing so, we dare to enter into the world of beyond both in language and in everyday awareness.

So in order to even understand what consciousness is one has to enter into it and use intuitive, insightful, so-called spiritual feeling in order to get a glimpse of the beyond that is here and now and everywhere, and is beyond formed language. Consciousness is composed of a very high frequency and high vibratory pulsating. It has to lower this state of vibration in order to densify into form which consists of a lower vibrational energy. The more formed the creation, the more dense its energy.

Human beings therefore vibrate at a low density pulsation whilst butterflies pulsate at a higher tone. Animals, quite like humans in their earthiness, have a low pulsating energy. This does not mean that there is a hierarchy of vibration; it simply means one is less imbued with physicality than the other. Of course it also means we have a more complex brain capacity and more complex physicality which can be used to create a more intricate and integrative life.

The pure will or imaginative thought of the oversoul, already existing within consciousness, individuates and propels consciousness to form, thus to the proliferation of created phenomena. Electric energy is being attracted and magnetized to earth by the soul energy. So the will to earth is what guides consciousness in the trajectory of earthing. In other words, consciousness is directed by willpower to earth. It is never altered or changed within itself by incarnation, rather it remains itself before and after, during and beyond creative impulses. It always was and always will be consciousness.

As I mentioned, the reptilian brain helps us humans to automatically adapt to our environment. It helps us to survive on the earth plane and created a space for consciousness to adapt to the human environment. Our ancestors did not possess the complexities of thought and intellect that centuries later we, their offspring, possess in our three-brain scenario. With this progress we are able to make decisions based on compassionate principles rather than on principles of survival.

This also gives us more responsibility to choose wisely and live honourably in our various communities. The opening of our heart to our self and one another has come through centuries of evolutionary thought and adaptation to our physical environments to include our own physical bodies.

Alice Bailey stated that before birth, that great agent of consciousness, a particular soul animated by divine impulse (DNA) and beyond mere human brain capacity saw the perfect state in which to be birthed. It realized how a particular environment on the earth plane could support its human journey to evolve even further in its spiritual evolution. Particular parents on an energetic level were asked if they might be willing to cater for this soul's earth journey. Consent being given, the soul was propelled by consciousness into form. Often, if a being decides to earth too quickly after death, this being is usually ego-driven.

Plato's belief in a blueprint for all physicality suggests that the physical organs of the body together with the various systems and automatic impulses, also possessed this perfection, and this is individual for each being. We each have our own journey to reach our divine being-ness. My organs in my body are vibrating at a frequency perfect for me.

Each organ in the body has its own peculiar vibratory pulse, peculiar to that person and their resonances and vibrations are affected by their particular thoughts, emotions and traumas. This blueprint or template is like an energetic sheath around each organ and body system. One cannot see it, but energy workers can have a felt sense of it. Some modern scientists refer to it as an aura or glow. This is the electromagnetic pulsating created by the individual soul's state of awareness and it changes with each incarnation.

One can deduce that our organs and internal systems have been chosen by our soul to fit our incarnational journey which will of course change with each evolutionary shift. In the end, as we progress on our journey, we shall become lighter in physicality as our earth-mindedness will have become imbued more and more with consciousness. When one decides to donate an organ at death, it is well to go beyond mere physical reasons and confused earth-guided love to do so. If we do not wish to get involved with karmic responsibility of another it's important to think things through from the soul aspect. One has to look at the energetic principles at work.

Spiritual ethics are not considered these days and so we are driven by a false sense of compassion to give parts of ourselves to strangers or family, forgetting that the auric sheath surrounding each of our organs contain our experiences, our emotions and our thoughts. The body is a holographic entity; change one part and all parts are affected.

When a heart is removed at brain death to facilitate another body to continue living, it is still pulsating with the particular vibration of the one who died. The aura surrounding it is severed in a traumatic way so that it cannot unite with the Universal Heart. This is a very serious consideration not known to many and certainly not acknowledged in the field of medicine. This trauma to the heart can affect the one receiving it and the energetic wounding can last for many incarnations. In this case often no cause will be found because people do not look to the energetic-spiritual reasons for illness.

As the astral body is the template for the whole body, it takes its time after death to dissolve naturally. If this is interfered with, as in organ donation, the soul cannot join with the astral, as soul will always go to source. Therefore the astral stays earth-bound and seeks another form to inhabit, usually that of a relative with similar life beliefs.

The astral carries the emotional residue of the life lived and if the emotions were healed into unconditional love, the inner marriage of soul and astral takes place. With organ transplantation, great inner confusion is still felt in the astral body. More can be read about this in my book *Celtic Wisdom in Contemporary Living.*

Dying as Preparation for Further Living

Live dear one
Live as though the next in-breath
Like the finest wine
Whilst leaving its red dew on your mouth
At the same time hastens to leave

144

Savour each breath
With the passion of a lover
Knowing that in the breath
Of every kiss
There is the movement of its passing.

If we were fully alive and consciously aware during earth life, of letting breath in and letting it leave easily, we would not be afraid to live passionately. We would have great energy for all our experience of life without labelling these experiences as good or bad or sad or joyful. What seems to prevent us from fully living is that we tend to hold on to life as if it were going to end! What is life anyway, but a wondrous preparation, like an initiation for yet another experience of living. We do literally "pass over" and in Gaelic we call it "trasna". I love this word trasna. We go beyond this experience of life to another experience of life. *Trasna dia fein* meaning "beyond God itself", we go on into eternity, into our mystery. Then we will have our inner eye opened and see for the first time that what we called the end was but a rest and a pause between breaths.

For life as I see it is the mighty spiritual force, the force in which we dance the spiral of creation with all life. We continue in that spiralling movement dancing here and there, and here becomes there and in the end there is neither here nor there but a glorious presence, infiltrating the whole gamut of being. Imagine, dear one, being so lifted into Love or life that in the end our coming is our going and our going is our coming again.

Language fails to describe what I often experience when I'm in Love or fully engaged with life. It is a falling into Love, down from the judgments and smallness of the earth mind and a sinking into the very womb of God and seeing everything and all through the eyes of pure life or Love. As I experience it, the death experience is another trasna preparing me for another dance with Love and life. The Aíte of life I see is preparing me for life within form and then when I leave form I'm invited to trasna once more into pure energy. This experience prepares me for life without form and here I learn even more about the mystery of life and Love.

When the two become one there is no difference between life and Love, for they will have embraced one another as in the kiss I spoke about in the poem above, and that kiss too, is transitory. It is always in the movement of passing, the movement of trasna. So for me the spiral of becoming is non-stop experiencing of Love in its various evolutionary stages, from human conditional love to pure life force neutral Love. The deeper I grow into pure Love the deeper my compassion and capacity for human love. The deeper I grow into human love the deeper my gratitude for the grace of divine Love. And I live each day breathing in, breathing out, living and dying.

The Devotion of an Anam-Áire

Following, the expressions *soul* and *life force* are interchangeable:

The word Anam-Áire is an Irish word meaning carer for the soul. Another translation is watcher with the soul as in watching with the living and dying. In ancient Ireland the Crones, ie., the older women in the community, were the watchers with birth and death. They were known also as the Seabheanna or old wise women in the community. The younger women could always confide in such women and get good advice when they had problems. It was said that these older women were (from the Irish):

> comh aosta mar na sleibhte
> comh comhfiosach mar an beatha
> comh fiochmhar mar an gaoth
> comh sobhriste mar anail leanbh
>
> as ancient as the mountains
> as conscious as life
> as fierce as the wind
> as fragile as the breath of a child

In being called to help a woman at childbirth the Anam-Áire was chosen for her:

- ability to focus;
- ability to be fully present to what was presented in that moment;
- ability never to distract from watching with soul coming or going;
- ability to never judge the experience;
- ability to never lose her breath or be dismayed, knowing that the soul knows its own trajectory and that her devotion is to follow the soul's lead;
- ability to remain neutral no matter what occurs. This state of neutrality was known as soul compassion without emotional discharge.

The natural trajectory of soul coming into form is one of travelling from the top of the head down through the coccyx towards the feet. The natural trajectory of soul leaving form is from the feet upwards to the top of the head.

When assisting at a birth the Anam-Áire concentrated her energy at the top of the baby's head and blew a breath to this area as it appeared, thus supporting the soul to travel to the feet and ground life force, ie., cathex. At a death she reversed the action by blowing her breath to the feet, thus supporting soul to leave the form, ie., to decathex or unground life force.

When mother had had time to bond with the child through touch, voice and feeding, father then took the child in his arms and with his mouth on the fontanelle of the baby's head, he breathed into it, welcomed and named the child and bonded with it by touch and voice. The community later came with gifts of soul for the child and mother. Such gifts might have included for instance the gift of long life, of good health, laughter, strong breath, ability to sing to the wind, good relationship with the animal kingdom etc.

In watching with the dying the Anam-Áire travels with soul to the other dimensions of energy. This she does by closing her eyes and concentrating, focusing on the energy field around the dying person.

As the consciousness of the dying person expands far and beyond the confinement of the room, the Anam-Áire is able to track the energy field that is leaving form and supports it on its journey to its chosen further life experiences as an energetic being. These are dictated by life choices. She can detect if the journey becomes erratic or if blocks appear in the energy field from the first energy centre situated near the coccyx, right through to the top of the head.

Whilst watching with the dying I have observed how if the natural flow of energy gets stuck in the lower fields this prevents the life force or soul from departing form with a peaceful flow. When this happens I use sound as a support to decathexing. The sound I emit is of a low frequency at first, growing into a higher one as the energy is released.

If people watching with the dying cannot make the sounds, I advise them to whisper the mantra, "That too is flowing upwards."

These words can be said by anyone sitting by the dying as long as they are not emotionally involved with the person dying. Many dear people carry guilt from past deeds and are unable to forgive themselves or another. When self-forgiveness is experienced, life force is helped to travel up the energy fields and integrate any unfinished business leaving the being with inner calm and peace.

When I experienced an NDE in 1973, I observed from my bed how the energy in my body expanded out beyond the hospital room. It was as though the shock had driven the life force out of my body. But this was not so. If the life force had left completely I would have died. I now believe that what I was experiencing was the astral body journeying outside. This we do in dream time also of course. So, when I hear people say their soul left their body I find this difficult to hear because when that happens we are no longer around to tell the story!

If you are with someone who is dying, do not sit too close to the bed. It is good to be fully calm and without words, other than those advised above. Words often distract and bear no witness to the inner journey of the dying. Just be present without sound, that is also an amazing gift. Remember the dying person is absorbing the atmosphere and the energy around them, yours too, so your calm state of non-judgment and non-emotional heart-watching will be a source of support to them.

Singing for the dying has been used as an aid to the soul departing. I spoke with the well-known Therese Shroueder-Shaker who developed music-thanatology at the end of the last century (music for the dying). This involved singing a variety of higher octave sounds with harp accompaniment for the dying and Therese used what was known as monastic medicine, using Latin instead of English words. This music does not have a discernible beat. It is free flowing and is not the usual rhythmic music we know. This practice is done with great awareness and consciousness of the soul leaving form. Therese, like me advises that to do this devotion one needs to have worked much on their own dysfunctional psychological patterns. One needs to die many times in the day to their own experiences and be comfortable with the thought of one's own death in order to devote time and energy to the dying. Any deaths in one's family not grieved fully also need attending to.

My own Celtic practice is very akin to what Therese teaches and we shared time discussing similarities. Like Therese, I do not agree with the use of everyday words as they often keep the soul grounded, keep it curiously involved with earth life. For example, if a song has a certain rhythm and the words are sentimental, this does not help the soul to depart but keeps it attuned to the earth experience. What we might consider lovely, healing words such as "we remember you, God loves you, go home, part of our family, we love you, sleep dear one, be happy" etc., may create distraction and prevent the soul from focusing on the inner journey and the inner adventure. Words ground in this given reality whilst various sounds emitted at the right time support the dying in theirs.

I usually close my eyes, humble myself in front of such a magnificent mystery and allow intuitive awareness to create appropriate sounds. And the sounds are always different no matter how many times I sound them. They come from an altered state of consciousness and as such are intuitive and always fresh. In the olden days in Ireland they were named Gutha, meaning simply, sounds.

We have to use the deepest humility as we watch with the dying. We are involved with mystery and we have no right to delve too far into the unknown with such limited awareness of what spirituality really is. This inner state of humility can help us to be open to what is, and not think we know all the answers. Just as birthing is a deeply spiritual experience, so is death as well. Silence near the birthing bed and silence near the dying bed are needed if the life grounding and departing are to be supported by the community.

Questions to Explore

- What is longing to be given life through you?
- What thought patterns do you have to release in order for the dream to happen?
- What is the dream you dream but dare not live?
- Have you ever thought about what happens to the form at death?
- Would you want to donate your organs after you die?
- Would you receive an organ from another?
- What would you like your death to be like?
- Do you believe we choose our own deaths?
- Do you see how birth and death are similar?
- What do you believe happens after you die? Is it the end?

Chapter V

Questions and Answers

Remember
Did you not know?
You are the bird
Tumbling from the throat of love
Did you forget?
That we have come
To earth the divine
In your heart and mine
You're not alone
Your tiny boat
Though battered
Has still braved the storm
You have come home
All of yourself
Is now gathered in
To love again.

Let these words of wisdom from my friend Jules Harrington touch your lovely hearts and let you know that you are loved into life and death.

There is no power more powerful than you
no love more loving than you
no wisdom more wise than you
Let that shake your branches.
Let the truth of that
pull the dry leaves of your misunderstanding
to the ground
Let the children dance on them to dust
and now look at you, stripped naked of your confusion
like a tree in autumn all rooted in truth
with silvery skin standing strong. *SEÁ*

b elow are some of the questions I have been asked throughout the years regarding death and helping the dying:

Q: Who dies?
A: The personality; the ability to be a person again in this life time, in this body, is what dies.

Q: What goes beyond death?
A: The divine energetic being that I am will never die. It is energy and energy transforms. It can be transmuted and it can be used and abused, but it cannot die as it does not have a personality in and of itself.

Q: Why do we all fear death?
A: We fear death because we find it difficult to experience change. Change belongs with the unknown, the dark. It is something elusive. Religions have not made it easy for us to look on death with anything other than fear. The idea of a judging God ready to condemn us to hell because we have not lived up to his standards does not help. Neither does the image of purgatory make the dying process any easier. According to the Catholic faith I learnt as a young child, purgatory is a place for waiting on God's mercy to release us from a state of darkness. I have found that many religious people themselves have a fear of dying and are not fit to help their flock when it comes to their dying process. Neither do I know many medical people who have actually studied death as such in any detail, other than the medical model of extinction, a medical model of brain death.

Of course when one is twenty-years-old, one does not want to speak about death and dying, yet we will all experience death at some time, so it is a good and healthy thing to include it at times in our conversations about life.

Q: What helps the dying to die peacefully?

A: Often I have seen that what may be a happy, peaceful dying process for one person might not be for another. Just as our birthing processes are different so will our dying processes be. Some people love to have music sung to them when they are in pain and others do not want to hear it. We have to listen to the dying person and not impose a so-called happy death on them. Some people may have been very religious all their lives but when they were dying they did not want to hear prayers or holy mantras.

Be led by the dying person and ask questions whilst they can still communicate as they are the experts. Do not wait until they can no longer answer questions if there are important answers you need. If possible, communicate well before the person is on their dying bed. Ask questions like: What kind of burial do you want? What do we do with your precious things? Who would you choose to officiate at your ceremony, if you want to have one? I recommend the book *Before I Go* by Jane Duncan Rogers. Jane leaves no question unanswered.

Q: Is it good to have candles and flowers and photos in the room of a dying person?

A: My answer is no. It is easy for the astral being to attach itself to material things that used to delight them. Smells can be very magnetic and can draw the energy back to earth. Candles also give off a light and a smell that can be distracting to the dying person. Let there be a minimum of furniture and artefacts in the room. In the old days in Ireland, all mirrors, photos, flowers, candles were removed during the last hours. Windows were shut and people left the room and closed the door. This was all done to facilitate the soul's departure. Here is an old poem that advised:

> Take my photo off your wall
> Lest I in deep sleep
> Slip back into the memory
> And make it my resting place.

Take my candle from its nest
And blow it out lest I
In search of light
Might bind into its haunting charms.
Then take yourself my love
And hide away for fear
That I in death's last grasping breath
Perchance might cling to yours.

Q: Is it helpful to keep holding a dying person's hand and speak to them as they die?

A: There is a time and a place for all things. A time to hold a hand, a time to not hold a hand. It depends on the stage of dying. It is for me always the better option to invite the person to hold your hand if that is what would help them, rather than going ahead and just holding their hand. When the person is not able to respond either verbally or symbolically by moving an eyelid or finger, I do not offer this. If you can imagine that the consciousness of the dying person expands into the room, the house and even the surrounding district then their physicality is ultra-sensitive. And so, to hold a hand at this stage, when the elements are dissolving, would not be helpful. It is better to withhold from touching as much as possible.

When the fire energy is dissolving, the body is on fire so touch would not be appropriate. A very light piece of cotton wool, cool to the touch but not cold, might be applied gently to the forehead. Never should cold water or cold touch be applied as that creates shock to the system. As hearing is the last sense to leave, I often said the words, "You are not alone, whoever you'd like to be with you just call them to you." Often at this stage of dying the dying begin to manifest their dead relatives that they loved and they appear to them in a very comforting way.

Usually I'll have discussed all this with the person before they get to the last stages of dying. I have had many wonderful, inspiring conversations with people whilst they were able to comprehend the meaning of the words and when they were dying I would follow their instructions. I remember one old man telling me that he wanted to be reminded to ask his dead sister to come and help him to "get to the other side of the mountain". I'm sure she was there because the smile of recognition was on his face as he breathed out his last breath.

Here are the words of a song I often record for people who are afraid at the moment because they are going through the pain and exiled experience of being in hospital with the Covid-19 virus. It seems to be helping in a small way.

> You're not alone
> I'm watching here
> Breathe in the love
> Breathe out the fear
> My hand is near
> Beside your own
> Just feel it now
> That you're not alone
> You're not alone
> Though night has come
> Your angel friend
> Carries you home
> You're safe to leave
> And you're safe to stay
> Follow your soul
> She knows the way
> And you're not alone
> You're not alone.

It is important to remember that every sound and smell will be magnified in the mind and consciousness of the dying person. Please remember this as you sit with them. Remember also, as the consciousness is expanding they become clairaudient, clairvoyant and telepathic. So guard your thoughts well in the room of the dying. It can help to sit very quietly as in meditation repeating words such as:

> "Go softly dear one
> into the arms of peace
> soft gentle peace
> We let you go
> Your guardians are with you
> Go with our love and our blessings
> Your own ones are waiting for you
> the ones you loved on earth.
> They will help you now
> call on them."

Instant manifestation of intention is available to the dying and it is good to remind them of this. Many times I have said words like, "Go into the beautiful scenery you have imagined, see the water and the blue sky and dive into the blue ocean. You are safe, all is well." I have many, many times rehearsed with people what they want me to say to them as they are dying. I am often delighted that many people find these visualizations to be a greater comfort and help than imagining a God ready to judge them as they close their eyes in death. Maybe it is a good idea to start practising daily what you would like to manifest as you are dying! Of course life is the preparation and if we have the clarity of mind, the pureness of heart and there is no unfinished business to get in the way at this stage of dying, we can certainly enjoy a beautiful death. I wish this for us all and for all beings on the earth, now and for all times.

Q: If someone seems to be fidgeting and becomes irate what is this and how do I help?
A: This so-called fidgeting and irateness can sometimes have to do with the internal energetic exchanges that happen as the elements dissolve. Often a dying person may scratch at the

bedclothes and pull them with their hands. I have referred to this before at the stage when the fire is leaving. They may also scratch at their skin as it is now very dry. Often, light cotton gloves can help. I sometimes would apply a gentle moisturizer such as baby cream to hands before putting on gloves. This fidgeting could also be indicative of earth energy dissolving and they experience the sensation of falling down and they are trying to hold on. A gentle reminder that all is well, your angel waits for you, Love is surrounding you now, just sink into it. Your voice needs to be very soft and slow. Take your time, few words are needed. Your own breathing can be a huge help as the dying can be greatly affected by your breathing rhythms. I realized this when once I had been dealing with my own family difficulties while attending someone terminally ill but not quite at the dying stage. He knew by my breathing that something was out of balance in me! I remember him saying, "Are you alright this evening?" I answered saying, "I'm having a bit of a problem, but I'll be ok." He said, "Ah well, just breathe in slowly and you'll be fine!" It is wonderful when the dying help us! Just breathe softly, deep in your abdomen. I have always found it important to tell dying people the truth. They know anyway when we are trying to withhold it.

As the body loses its muscle power, the dying may also try to scratch their leg or arm as they have an itch and cannot scratch it, and this may leave them frustrated. To facilitate a deeper understanding of the needs of the dying I have used word cards and sentence cards, written in large print with questions such as "Do you need something?" I negotiate with the dying person when they are still able to communicate with me as to the ways and means whereby they can have needs met by means of these cards. The movement of a finger can mean yes, and the smallest movement of head can mean no in answer to a question on the card.

Also remember as life force is withdrawing, it can feel like a crawling sensation just under the skin. Bedclothes should be light cotton if possible, as contact with the skin can be uncomfortable.

It helps to lift up the bedclothes every twenty minutes as well as to apply a drop of water to the mouth and lips. You can buy swabs that have been moistened in glycerine and honey to moisten the mouth. When the fire energy is dissolving it's helpful to have a small noiseless fan, not an electric one, a little away from the bed. Always remember that the body/mind is ultra-sensitive as the life force is preparing to leave.

The least amount of interference with this spiritual passage is vital. Imagine then what it might be like to be given injections or drips at this time. To honour the earth body we need to respect its processes whether in life on earth or at the leaving stage. Too much cleaning of the body and too much speaking in the room about the dying patient can be truly intrusive.

Please never discuss the dying person with another, while in the room with them as if the dying person is not there. Often we tell lies to dying people as if that did not matter. I have heard many doctors say things to relatives in the corridor such as, "Oh, she is not doing well," and then go into the room of the dying and happily say, "You look much better today."

I believe in telling the truth both to relatives and to the dying themselves. And it is not conducive to a dignified death if we insist on giving the dying hope when none is evident. It is important that we honour the soul at all times. As an aside, the dying know they are dying but often join in the family lie that they are "just fine". This is frequent especially if the family practice is to hide the truth when it is not pleasant. So rather than go on with their own very important journey into death they caretake the relatives and try to act out their wishes.

Just as a newborn child needs a quiet, silent place wherein to come into the world, the dying need the same when about to leave. Imagine what a dying person goes through when she/he is being "brought back to life" several times. This strong medical intrusion upsets the entire psyche leaving the dying person shattered. To die with dignity is difficult if we are attached to machinery or being drugged so much, that we can no longer be consciously aware of our dying process. When we all understand that life is not dependent on form we will not try to hold on so much to earth life whether we are the one dying or the one left behind.

Q: Should I pray for my dying friend even though I am not of their religion?

A: Words that come from the heart of loving intention are always acceptable both to the ones on earth and to the ones leaving it. When I lived in Northern Ireland I attended some of the funerals from both Catholic and Protestant backgrounds. Many Protestants attended the mass and prayed for the dead friend and likewise the Catholics for their dead friends. I remember one woman asking me if I thought she might be allowed by the family to pray for the happy passing of her Protestant bingo friend. When I did ask the family the answer was so heartening. "Of course she must pray her prayers for our Teresa! Sure prayers from the heart of a friend are always heard." I have never forgotten the words of this wise Irish woman. The vibratory contents of heartfelt loving prayer soothes and offers solace both to the one praying and the one receiving these loving vibrations.

Q: How do I deal with a friend whose child is dying in hospital?

A: The way your own loving heart would deal with loss no matter what it is. You can be there for her if she needs to talk. Never give advice or say things like, "It is so sad that wee Mary is so ill, but I'm sure God will heal her", or "This is awful for you dear, but thank God she is so young you didn't get used to her around the house. It would be worse if she was older", or "Sure you can have another child. You are still a young woman, thank God."

Keep including the wee one in your conversations with your friend and make time for her to deal with the grief—not trying to calm her, distract her or make it better for her. You can't. Grief has her own timing. Grief is bigger than death. It goes on and on.

Sometimes it seems like it takes over. If we don't willingly give time for pain, she'll take it anyway. If you have not dealt with your own griefs in life you will not be able to stand your friend's grief. You will do all you can to make her smile again, and this does not help her nor does it honour the deep spiritual alchemy of grief.

It is good to offer practical help at times like this. Help the family by perhaps collecting other children from school, take them to your house and feed them. Clothes may need to be washed, ironed and the house may need to be hoovered and meals made. There are so many ways we can help at times like this. Always ask if there is a way you can help.

You do not have to be different with someone because they are dying or because their loved one is dying. Ask questions rather than assume anything. Just know that it is ok not to know what they need and it is also ok not to be able to provide it. All this is important when you sit with the dying and their families. Let the words of this song I composed in 2002 help your heart:

> I can't give you back your strength
> I can't give you back your breath
> I can't give you back the years to live again
> And I can't take away this pain.
> I can't make your dream come true
> I can't bring this life back to you
> I can't melt the ice of all the frozen years
> But I can hold you in your fears.
> Don't wait, I hear you say
> Until your dying day
> Before you do the things you want to do.
> Before your life is gone
> If there are things undone
> Do them now
> Say them now
> Live them now.

I can't go this road with you
This is something only you can do
I can give to you the only thing that's mine
I'll share with you my time.
I sit and watch with you
My tears are flowing
I sing my lullaby
This is goodbye.

Q: How can I learn about being with the dying and relatives?
A: The first thing is to be open, gentle and compassionate with yourself in times of grief, hurt and not knowing. As you are with your own vulnerability, you will be with another's. If you can be empathetic without entering into the pain of the other that will be a great help to them. When we do our own grief work we can sit with another and be a blessing. If you sit and cry with your dying friend each time you are with them you can't hear what they try to tell you. You can't be present to their pain and fear if you have not been present to your own.

Dear one, if you are to be with the dying then you need to have truly experienced your own loss and pain and have been able to go through the stages of grief so that there is a free space in you to sit quietly and just be. How have you reacted or responded to grief in your own life? Did you just survive it by being distracted or by not speaking about it, pretending it was not so awful? Did you work very hard so that you did not have to truly face it? Did you minimize your own grief and magnify others' so that you could feel better and not feel the wound? You will know the answers dear one and there is no blame. Of course there is never blame.

You always did the best you could with the knowledge you had at the time. This saying has always helped me in times of guilt in the past. To be able to let things be, without trying to fix anything or trying to be all things to all people can often be difficult for us. We have been trained to rescue and to caretake. This is how we got attention as a child and some of us still continue this into adulthood.

I have found that it is not so simple to sit quietly with full awareness and offer my full presence to the dying person but it is always enough.

Love flows between us like a healing balm, soothing, and somehow I found myself many times being inspired to whisper some words of comfort that seemed to touch the dying. From a place of uninterrupted watchfulness, soul has room to speak through us as the earth mind is stilled into silence and awe.

In this sacred space we breathe the divine and are met with pure love that heals and so death can be the ultimate healer.

> Who died they asked the old one
> For the house was in strange quiet
> After the wake
> Some body died indeed, said she
> Cackling to herself
> Behind her white clay pipe
> Sure isn't it only
> The tired flesh of years
> Crept back into the clay
> But the life of herself
> Now dances a fairy reel
> And God and Brigid smiling on her… *SEÁ*.

Postscript

When exploring the themes of this book with others, through my workshops, a question that often comes up is what happens in the event of a sudden death. When a sudden death happens it is a severe shock to the whole nervous system and yet I have written that sudden death also has its own timing. Although all internal systems would seem to shut down quickly, to trained perception this is not so and although the heart may have stopped pulsating, there is an energy that remains in the energetics as the heart template is still present. It is as though deep compassion holds the system in deep presence. It is my belief that even the suddenness of a death serves the story of the departed. We do not know the story that brought that being to Earth therefore we cannot judge its leaving.

For certain the elements have had no time to dissolve slowly, as is their wont, and they have to adapt very quickly to dissolution which can have the effect of a bang going off inside. The elements that held the the physicality together have been shattered at an unnatural speed. This leaves the psyche confused, shocked and in a state of not knowing if death has happened or not.

Suicide has the same effects on the Psyche. Prayers of Intercession are important as are calming sounds with a high octave voice. I used to sing thus; wordless tones and gently interspersing sound with Celtic Mantras.

This subject deserves more than I can allow here. Maybe my next book will be more informative.

Phyllida

Celtic Blessings and Poems

Poetry for me is a safe and honourable container for soulful communication. Poetry imagines what my cognitive mind finds difficult to articulate. From a place of depth and other-worldliness I find poetry sings the Universe alive for me; takes mere words to a heart opening space in the imagination. Below are some some of these imaginative spaces that may also help bring the Universe alive for you too.

Celtic Soul Awakeners
Look deeper than the face of things
There you will find the timeline of its birth
Be not content with quick known answers
They do not serve the deeper life.
These curiosities do not need answers.
The answers lie in the silence between heartbeats
Which in turn will ask a different question
Answer from joy, not from pain
As the pain will rob the answer of wisdom
And give it a problem instead.

Beauty
Live the beauty you are
Go deeper into the inner country
And find landscapes that until now
Offered no shelter
My friend, have a will to find
The beauty of your own heart-print in all.

Death Song

Know dear ones,
The song of death sings
At the centre of all creation
As the beloved embraces your heart
You are preparing for her to leave.
In the centre of the seed
Hides the mystery of creation
In the same centre dwells
The destroyer of all that is created.
So live with the companionship of death
And die fully alive.

An End to the Practice

Practise humility.
Practise silences.
Practise loving.
Practise delight.
And when you have practised,
Burn the teaching.
Scatter the pages to the five directions.
And when you have danced on the ashes of your passion
Feed the practices with your own breath
To the hearts of those to follow.

The Completion of Love

As the spiral is the completion of the circle
So too are you the completion of love
For God was an incomplete mystery
Until you grounded yours.
Your happiness, dear sister, is momentary
For it is easily eaten up by time
Your joy however, finds its breath in eternity
For its companion is soul.

Ecstatic Living

You say all that is presented to you
Comes from the hands of God
Then let your unease teach you
Just how far you live from ecstasy.

Live Joyfully

Practise mercy
Until it flows into compassion
Then give up the practice
And live joy.

Opening Deeper

And when you keep answering
The call of grief
You open deeper into the raw barren fields
Of brokenness
And gather all suffering
Into the spaces
That grief has widened in you.
Weep not for the ones who will not carry grief
But lay it at your heart door
Offer it back to them
Like daisies from the field
In humble renunciation.

No Escape

And in your sorrowing
Become one with nature
And howl your nakedness
To the wounded leaves in winter.
Do not say spring is not far off
But keep company with a songless bird
As she mourns with toneless throat
The death of her children.

Living Sacrament
The more times I am with you
the more myself I become
you carry in and about you a divine ease
so beautifully crafted to form
you need not speak one word,
your silences heal.
And when you do,
the stillness between words
brings me balm
and I am wrapped in devotion
of you; you a living sacrament
that teaches without words
that elevates without movement
Please show me what you know.

Timing
There is a timing in all things
There is a wisdom in nature's timing
Hold her hand and let her show you this day.
And when you fast as the brothers fast
Do so with no thought of sacrifice
No god to sacrifice your bread to
Only the joy of knowing
If your body needs the bread you will serve it
As you would serve the Christed one.
Let your fasting then be not in sacrifice
But let the body be made
Even more sacred in the cleansing.

Triple Flame

The triple flame of your heart
Burns for the sacred making of desires
So that the love you live
May spread like wild-fire
Scorching all beings, even *tighe* (the cat) in its trail.

Rename the Sacred

Let all that needs to be made sacred in you happen in this breath
Not when you lay breathless in death
Now is the day to rename the sacred everywhere.
What you believe to be sacred, is indeed so.
For no one can name the sacred for you.
Nor can it be taken from you.

The Choice

If love be not your deepest desire
Then dear one
Die now and come again when you are ready
To choose life
For until you choose
You will be troubled
And will be a trouble.

A God to Trust

Tell me about your god
does she tell stories
does she sing
does she laugh loudly
and does she warm her feet by your hearth?
If so, then I will listen to her truths.

Religion

A religion that does not include story telling
is not a religion at all
but a strict, fixed glue-tight set of rules
and fear-filled commandments
used only to underpower,
undermine and manipulate.
The inclusion of story
softens theology
humanizes precepts
upholds mysticism
And attracts soul.

Your Dying

When your own song seduces you
Back into that symphony again
Let your throat widen into eternity
And rent the seas apart with the force of your passion
So that life may play the strings of your soul
In total magnificence. *SEA.*

Feed Your Soul

Whatever delights your heart, feeds your soul
See how your soul sickens because of malnourishment
You would feed the animals in the farmyard
You would play with the streams and sing to the mountains
You delight in the passions of sunsets
And rise early to kiss the dawn
You embrace your sister after an hour missing from your eyes.
Yet your own heart faints and pales
Because of no attention and no hearth blessings.

The Neutrality of Life

Life is neutral in its compassion
It has no agenda for you
Save the one you yourself signed
With the breath of your own life.
Love is neutral in its agenda for you
Save the one you chose
So that you could live it fully.
Death is neutral; it obeys your own timing.
You bring the breath, you live life through it.
Your date of death is written in your own script, no one rules over
you save at your own bidding.
And you would cry and shout, "Life is a hard ship, the seas are
dark and dangerous, my small boat is uneasy and death creeps
up on the side of my boat ready to take me to its dark."
Dear one you have been sleeping on the boat.
Time to awaken now.

All Is Information

All is information
You put the story together from past experiences.
Be curious about life,
Not judgmental
Otherwise the judgments will override the joys.
Gather yourself in,
All experience is an invitation
To live more fully
To love more ridiculously
And to die, singing a love song to yourself.

The Invitation
Life is an invitation, it is vital to live without boundaries
So that you may be free to walk the five directions without fear.
In the beginning of your adventure into the wild forest of life,
It is necessary to build boundaries
So that you may know your own limits
And so that others may also know theirs
Let your sight be on a boundless living into full joy.
Let your own breath flow
Like the seven rivers of mercy
Throughout the meadows and fields
The rivers and mountains
The valleys and hilltops
The ditches and swamps
The hideouts and homesteads
Of your own naming
So that at the End Day
You no longer yearn
For the outer landscape
In that glorious morning
This be your homeland that greets you.

Gathering In (by Louise Firetree, 2019)
We are gathering in
Welcoming all the parts
Those soul fragments
Left out in the dark
The unconscious
Is brought into consciousness
The unspoken
Is brought into awareness
That which is broken
Can be mended
Awakening to life
Lying in tenderness.

Glossary

Aíte (ahtcha): passageways or space to experience further

Anam-Áire: one who cares for the soul

Auric body: the energetic template for physical body

Cathexis: grounding

Cauldron of Brigid: symbol for life itself or soul where all is stirred without judgement; the equalizer

Celtic teachings: referring to teachings from the Cauldron

Clay body: physical body

Corpa bailligaigh: being non-fragmented, being gathered in, integrated

Decathex: leaving earth energy

Earth/ego mind: the consciousness we need to survive on earth

Gutha (guha): sounds referring to Celtic mantras

Hieros Gamos: internal integration, sacred inner marriage

Love: the Love, non-emotional, non-judgmental

Seá: meaning yes, so it is, amen.

Sacred Heart: another word for true compassion

Ujjayi breath: yogic sounding breath

Universal Heart: also Sacred Heart, heart of the creator, non-physical, non-emotional. When we have opened our own energetic heart into self-compassion which includes non-judgment, we open into the Universal Heart that carries all human experience with pure Love.

Acknowledgements

True gratitude to Ems Harrington without whose loving encouragement, editing, organizing contents, nudging and creative input, this book would never have reached completion. You guided me when it all seemed too much. Without your input in those early days Ems, I would not have finished this book.

Then came Greta Pattison with her endless patience as she saved chapters for me as my computer had forgotten how to save!! Thank you so much dear Greta.

And continued thanks to Sabine Weeke at Findhorn Press. What a journey we have experienced together since back in 2005. You helped transform my notebook scribbles then into *A Celtic Book of Dying*.

My true thanks to Morticia Crone for her professionalism and creative directness in script-reading and general editing, before Michael Hawkins received the manuscript, for final editing. Morticia's precise input added to the overall integration of the work.

And lastly, it was a joy to exchange life stories with Michael Hawkins. His feedback was gentle, open hearted, delightful and everything just flowed with ease.

I send blessings of abunDance to you all.

About the Author

Photo by Bill Cunningham

Phyllida Anam-Áire grew up in a small village in Donegal, Ireland, born into a family traumatized by grief from loosing two of her siblings. In the 1960s, she spent her formative adolescent and young adult years as a Catholic nun in Dublin. Going on to raise a family in Northern Ireland with her Protestant husband of 26 years during the "Troubles", Phyllida was no stranger to death on a daily basis.

Her work with the dying, most especially her ten years working with Elisabeth Kübler-Ross, M.D., in the U.S. and Europe, mapped out her life. Having spent the last 40 years working as a psychotherapist, a continuous theme for Phyllida's retreats and gatherings is "Living Consciously into Death".

Her deep Celtic roots provide a strong creative ground for Phyllida's music and poetry. The author of *A Celtic Book of Dying*, she has published several books and music CDs and teaches the old Celtic Rituals and Gutha, Irish mourning sounds or mantras.

Phyllida believes that her greatest achievements are her two adult children, Anthea and Richard, and she loves being a grandmother. She lives in Edinburgh, Scotland.

You can contact Phyllida at: **seabheann@icloud.com**

FINDHORN PRESS

Life-Changing Books

Learn more about us and our books at
www.findhornpress.com

For information on the Findhorn Foundation:
www.findhorn.org